UP WHERE YOU BELONG

UP WHERE YOU BELONG

A GOD'S EYE VIEW DEVOTIONAL

TOMMY TENNEY

THOMAS NELSON PUBLISHERS®
Nashville

A Division of Thomas Nelson, Inc.
www.ThomasNelson.com

ISBN 0-7852-6561-9

Printed in the United States of America
02 03 04 05 07 BVG 6 5 4 3 2 1

To a special young girl
who I know will be lifted up
where she belongs.

CONTENTS

CONTENTS

CONTENTS

CONTENTS

UP WHERE YOU BELONG

"Pick Me Up, Daddy!"
"I Can't See from Down Here"

Pressure tends to force honesty to the surface. Many who live in supposedly modern cultures carefully cultivate facades of self-sufficiency, self-reliance, and even deception and defiance . . . until they run into something that brutally brushes aside every frail human pretense toward God. In such moments of truth, the reality of dire human need cannot be denied.

Day 1

Trapped and Pressed on All Sides

My memory holds some clear snapshots of the look on my young daughter's face when we stepped into a hotel elevator to go downstairs. Everything was fine until that luxurious but limited space started getting crowded. It seemed that at every floor someone tried to squeeze themselves in.

Some people battle a fear of close places well into maturity, but the concern is universal among members of our knee-high population. (God's Eye View, pp. 1–2)

SCRIPTURE READING
2 Corinthians 4:8–9, in which Paul the apostle assures us he knew that "crowded" feeling very well (long before modern elevators existed).

PAUL THE APOSTLE described the dilemma in detail when he said, "We are hard-pressed on every side, yet not crushed; we are perplexed, but not in despair; persecuted, but not forsaken; struck down, but not destroyed."[1]

Most of the time we use the word *but* to add a negative condition or excuse to something we've said. The apostle Paul listed all the negative circumstances he faced because of his bold life for Christ, and then imposed the truth of God's faithfulness on every one of those circumstances. This is a normal way of life for people who have God's eye view of their circumstances.

When you find that you have more bills than money at the end of your month (assuming you faithfully gave your tithes and other gifts), what kind of "but" will you add to your description of the situation?

Will you say, "And it doesn't look like things are getting any better either," or *"But God is my Source and my Provider. According to His Word, I will pay all my bills and have more left over to plant as seed as well"?*[2]

A survey of one week's news reports seems to imply that violence has become the world's favorite "sport," with Christians and inhabitants of the Western world ranking higher and higher on the "favorite victim" lists. *What additional comment would you add to this statement?* (Remember, Jesus said, "Out of the abundance of the heart the mouth speaks.")

Would you add, "I think I'll just stick close to home and make myself a small target," *or* "It sounds like a great time for the children of God to stand up in boldness and love the lost in Jesus' name. It is time for another supernatural expansion of the kingdom of God in the earth"?

Do you ever worry and fret about the future? Do you sometimes wish you could just "check out" and leave this world early? It is a good and godly thing to anticipate absolute union with God in heaven, but perhaps a peek at God's-eye view might help you take a stand for Him during your stay on earth:

> If anyone should have nightmares about the end times, it isn't your Father. The Creator of the cosmos hasn't spent a single feverish second struggling to figure out how He will finance the future. He isn't worried about how much they're going to give Him at the celestial pawn shop for His heavenly throne. I doubt that He is worried about any of the things that you and I worry about. (p. 4)

Remember God's answer to that sinking "trapped in an elevator" feeling next time you feel trapped and hard-pressed on every side. He will never leave or forsake you—He made a solemn promise to stay with you.[3] Next time you feel that unwelcome "spiritual claustrophobia" close in on you, remember this:

4

Worship permits you to see things as your heavenly Father sees them. It lifts you from the pit of humanity's problems to a higher and purer perspective from the seat of Divinity. The power of a higher perspective is accessed through worship. Worship will lift your spirit. Worship will change your destiny. Worship will rearrange your future. (p. 4)

PRAYER

Father, no matter how bad things look down here, You make me feel better every time I lift my eyes toward You. People may fail me or act thoughtlessly in ways that bring harm, but You are always faithful. I worship You and praise Your name, Lord. I'm glad that my future and my destiny are in Your hands, and not in the hands of any man or woman.

Day 2

Cosmic Checkmate Begins with Upraised Hands

The only being who should have recurring nightmares about the end times is Satan. The Scriptures tell us that God told Satan (in his serpent costume) and Eve, "From now on, you and the woman will be enemies, and your offspring and her offspring will be enemies. He will crush your head, and you will strike his heel."⁴ No wonder Satan craves a hard hat!

Satan is intimidated by anyone who isn't afraid to bruise his heel in the process of crushing Satan's serpentlike head. Yes, a heel bruise may make you limp, but a crushed head is fatal. He cringes over the possibility that you may discover your God is bigger than every demonic image or scheme he conjures up.

He fears the day you shed your limited concepts of God and allow worship to elevate your perspective. The enemy dreads the moment worship causes you to lift your hands up to the One he fears above all others. He knows the game is up the moment your heavenly Father lifts your perspective into the heavenlies for a new view of life's low-level landscapes. (God's Eye View, p. 5)

SCRIPTURE READING
Revelation 1:17–18, where Jesus Christ describes the trophies of His cosmic checkmate and eternal defeat of Satan and his fallen followers.

CHESS IS AN ANCIENT GAME of strategy, where well-established winning moves begin long before the final move of a game piece locks the loser in the inescapable bondage of "checkmate."

Chess masters don't focus solely on the move at hand; they rack their brains to anticipate the moves of an equally clever opponent far in advance. The goal is to look beyond the pressures on one move to correctly perceive the final move before your opponent does.

Has it occurred to you that the God of "yesterday, today, and forever" has a distinct advantage over the adversary in virtually every area of spiritual conflict? He doesn't have to "guess" or gamble about the enemy's moves or strategies. He knows them even before the twisted thoughts enter the adversary's pride-swollen head.

How should this crucial piece of information change the way you play out the game of life?

Would you say you win by aggressively advancing on the enemy with all your strength and wisdom, or by "stretching your arms to the heavens in the universal sign of surrender and desperation"? (p. 2)

When Jesus said, "I am the First and the Last. I am He who lives, and was dead, and behold, I am alive forevermore . . . And I have the keys of Hades and of Death," was He saying He had already *won the match of the universe* or that He was *barely holding His own* from day to day?[5]

The practical truth is that life can get very complicated at times. What is the best thing you can do when you feel overwhelmed?

Should you "act like an adult" and fake your way through until everything collapses, or should you raise your arms to your Father with the heart and adoration of a child? Which posture and plan does the enemy of your soul fear the most? (Which act makes Satan run for a hard hat?)

PRAYER

Heavenly Father, I thank You for the strength and wisdom You've given me. I thank You for every natural ability, skill, and gift You deposited in my life, but what I really want and need is You. No matter how much I

---

educate, train, and improve my abilities or skills, I still want to be with You. I want to see things from Your point of view, within "touch distance" of Your presence. I lay down my strengths and empty my ego of self-reliance because I want to face this day in total reliance upon You.

Day 3

"I Don't Like the Way Things Look Down Here . . ."

In a sense, the problems we face as adults often make us feel like three-year-olds in an elevator crowded with big people and very large purses and briefcases. You may feel the birth pangs of faith rising up in your heart right now. The Holy Spirit is saying to you, Worship your way out of your circumstances.

If you don't like the way things look "down here," then change your perspective. (*God's Eye View*, p. 7)

SCRIPTURE READING

Ephesians 2:4–7, where we find God's seating instructions for the trip called life. (God reserved you a seat in a heavenly place right beside Jesus, with a window view of eternity.)

HARD TIMES have a way of "putting you in your place" of humility without any regard for all the adult achievements, honors, and credentials you've accumulated. How many times have you seen movies or news clips about "Skid Row" residents in large cities who were failed stockbrokers, educators, politicians, scientists, doctors, or destitute former millionaires?

What do you do when the walls of circumstance begin to close in and make you feel suddenly "small"? Do you live at the mercy of life's messes? Do you struggle hopelessly under the shadow of past failures and future fears? *Did you forget your holy house key?*

God has given you the key—*worship* can take you to a completely different understanding and lift you to a new plane of reality. Worship allows you to look from the seat of divine reality at what earth calls reality and say with certainty, "That isn't really real. Everything of this earth is going to pass away. It's only temporary."

What is really *real?* God and His Word. He said, "The grass withers, the flower fades, but the word of our God stands forever."⁶ *Too many times we allow fear to morph the weeds of life into paralyzing images of the dragons in dark dreams of defeat. Isn't it about time for us to stand on the Word of God more than we stand on circumstances?* (p. 7)

Many of the movies depicting times of war over the last one hundred years include chaotic scenes of traffic moving in two directions along the same road.

The largest traffic flow nearly clogs the road as people *flee the battle* using any means available. A smaller but more determined and organized military convoy moves against the popular traffic flow *toward* the battle.

Imagine a lone soldier on foot who struggles to pass through the press of people, virtually unable to see beyond the faces of the crowd swirling around him. What would happen if a general leading a military convoy drove up and offered the soldier a ride if he would serve as an attaché for the leader?

The lone soldier would suddenly find he had a seat for the duration of the ride—a seat beside the commander with a full view of the goal and an inside track on the strategy and ultimate outcome of the battle.

Do you feel as if you are struggling to fulfill your destiny "on foot" while surrounded by a sea of obstacles obstructing your view? Is the press of humanity and anti-God culture streaming away from the purposes of God, threatening to carry you along with it?

*Your General is here. He has been looking for someone like you.*⁷ *He has a reserved seat at His Son's side with your name on it.* Will you *wait* upon Him with your worship?

PRAYER

Father, I don't like the way things look down here at the moment. I can't seem to see a thing—except for the obstacle blocking my way. I felt tall yesterday, but I feel very small today. Pick me up, Father. I love You and I desperately need You. May I ride with You from now on?

Day 4

"Why Does Everything Look Out of Focus?"

Worship is heaven's tool of choice for readjusting skewed human perspectives. Worship possesses a supernatural ability to correct our spiritual vision problems and bring everything into divine focus. If Daddy isn't worried, why should I feel discouraged? (God's Eye View, p. 8)

SCRIPTURE READING
1 Corinthians 13:12, where Paul describes the church's temporary vision problem to the church at Corinth.

IN APRIL OF 1990, NASA, America's space agency, proudly unveiled and launched the revolutionary new Hubble Space Telescope using the space shuttle. No one knew that technological marvel would develop two serious problems that endangered its reason for existence—a "vision" problem due to nearsighted and astigmatic lenses, and the inability to "flex its solar panels" toward the sun to recharge its batteries.[8]

These same problems seem to plague many Christians today. We try to fly high but our vision is still grounded by human limitations, and we quickly lose power because we are slow to flex our worship panels toward the Son.

Do you wonder at times if you will ever fulfill your destiny in Christ? If you suspect you need a heavenly readjustment for your "skewed human perspective," then worship Him. Worship will take you places you could never go on your own.

The problem isn't that you want to fly high—you were created to do just that. Most of us have serious perspective problems compounded by our failure to worship Him without reservation.

A skewed perspective makes every molehill of life look like an impassable mountain from hell.

> People look at Mount Everest and say, "Oh, look—it's *huge!*" They are right, I suppose, but anyone can board a jetliner and fly right over the earth's highest point and *look down on that mountain* from a far higher perspective. Size, mass, and height all seem to depend on the height of your vantage point. The elevation of your observation site determines whether you say you are looking "up there" or "down there." (p. 9)

PRAYER

Lord, it's hard to admit it, but my spiritual eyesight is poor at best. When I can see, it is only "in part" and very dim at times. I've decided to fix my eyes on You as I pursue Your presence with all my heart.

If all I can see are Your footprints before me, at least I know I'm going in the right direction. Be my vision, Lord; lift me up to where I belong, seated in heavenly places with You.

God's House of Bread Should *Attract* Customers, Not Turn Them Away!

A church leader and dear friend told me a story that arrested my attention recently. The associated churches in his state gather in his town for a large family camp every year, and the attendance just keeps growing year after year. He said that the proprietors of a family-owned restaurant in the area became so frustrated that they decided to close the doors for the duration of the event because they didn't want so many customers!

Pardon my ignorance on the subject, but I thought people opened restaurants, shops, stores, and other businesses specifically to attract customers. *What separates this story from a hundred other interesting tales of odd human behavior is its shocking similarity to the behavior of many churches today.* (God's Eye View, p. 12)

SCRIPTURE READING

John 6:57–58, where Jesus reveals that He is the living Bread from heaven, the Bread that causes those who receive it to live forever.

WHY WOULD A BREAD STORE with an unlimited and inexhaustible supply of living bread (the kind that imparts eternal life and blessing) try to limit the hunger of its customers or downplay the miraculous powers of its Divine product? Perhaps it is because we've neglected to restock our house with the fresh Bread of God's presence.

As I noted in *The God Chasers:*

> [God] has prepared a great table of His presence in this day, and He is calling to the Church, "Come and dine."

We ignore God's summons while carefully counting our stale crumbs of yesteryear's bread. Meanwhile millions of people outside our church walls are starving for life. They are sick and overstuffed with our man-made programs for self-help and self-advancement. They are starving for *Him,* not stories *about* Him. They want the food, but all we have to give them is a tattered menu vacuum-sealed in plastic to protect the fading images of what once was from the grasping fingers of the desperately hungry.[9]

The way to "restock" the church with fresh Bread from heaven is to *attend to the Divine Customer first!* Our programs may help people in this life, but only our Savior can help them in this life *and* in the life to come. A program didn't topple Saul the persecutor from his horse and transform him into Paul the apostle—it was the *shekinah* (or visible) glory of God Himself.

Are you willing to worship Him until the Bread of Heaven begins to fill your gatherings with His Divine presence? If you dare to do it, you should also be prepared for the inevitable crowds of the hungry who will be drawn by the fragrance of the fresh Bread of God's presence.

*If you chose to tend to your own needs like a preoccupied and self-centered waiter or waitress, then be prepared to see the Divine Customer go elsewhere—*along with the other customers His presence attracts.

Sometimes I am afraid that God is whispering to our deafened ears, *You might as well close down this service.* Why? We act as if we don't really want any interruptions from our Divine Customer. We are too busy blessing and congratulating one another on our funny stories, shallow sermons, gifted solos, and splendid choir renditions. We are irritated by every interruption that might pull us away from our coffeepot conversations. It's as if we've forgotten that His Word says, "Those who wait on the LORD shall renew their strength."[10] (p. 12)

The fragrance of Divine visitation begins to waft through the church the moment we take our eyes off ourselves and fix our gaze upon Him. The proof of Divine habitation will alert the region to the presence of true Bread from heaven once we learn how to wait upon Him first, last, and always.

PRAYER

Dear Lord, thank You for reminding me why You came and established the church as heaven's Fresh Bread shop for hungry souls. You are my first and most important Customer, and the most important thing I can offer You is my life as an act of continual worship. Then the Bread of Your presence will provide all the church needs to feed the hungry with manna from heaven.

Day 6
_____

"Forget the Popcorn and the Performance— Give Me His Presence!"

> *Too many of us treat church as if it was a movie theater complete with padded seats and popcorn. We expect to sit in comfort, undisturbed and unperturbed as if we were the customers and He was the Cosmic Performer. But the process demands that you wait on God through your worship (not merely the borrowed worship of others). (God's Eye View, p. 14)*

_____

SCRIPTURE READING
Psalm 103, which commands, "Bless the LORD, O my soul . . . ," rather than "Bless my soul, O my LORD."

_____

THIS IS THE SIXTH DAY of this devotional week. The number six has been called the biblical number of man, and that precisely defines the problem—too many of us in the church have carried our entertainment and sports-spectator habits into the house of God. We knowingly or unknowingly demand the same "service" and entertainment value that we expect to receive in a movie theater, theatrical performance, or sports event.

Have you ever caught yourself "watching" the church parade as a spectator rather than applauding the Head of the church as a worshiper?

The problem is that God is no performer. We did not and could not begin to "pay the price of admission" for what Jesus Christ accomplished for us. As we've noted many times before, God actually thinks church is about Him. If we serve Him with our praise and worship, then He will take delight in visiting us with His manifest presence again and again.

How do we set right what has been so wrong?

Begin to be more concerned about *His comfort* than about your own. Ask the Holy Spirit to *disturb and perturb you* about anything and everything that concerns the Father. Begin to love the things He loves and hate the things He hates.

Renew your mind to the true picture of God in His church—*we* are the *waiters* and He is the Divine Customer. It is *your turn* to minister to *Him* (don't leave this all-important job solely in the hands of a preacher or worship team). It takes a *church* in unity to welcome the glory of God into a city.

PRAYER

Dear Father, please forgive me for all the times I've entered Your gates as a spectator with ticket in hand. Today I enter Your gates with praise in my mouth and worship in my heart for You. I've come to worship You in Your presence, not to watch some spiritual performance. This time, I am more interested in being a blessing to You than in receiving a blessing from You.

Out with Pious Petitions, in with Passionate Praise and Fervent Pleas

We've become content to make do with the "lesser gods" of religious ritual, self-reliance, and a powerless form of godliness.

All of this suits us just fine until we find ourselves on a crowded elevator with no apparent place to go. We begin to feel a certain panic rising in our hearts as our vision is reduced by the pressing presence of instability, disease, tragedy, misfortune, or an outright assault by the adversary. In that moment, we drop all pretense of spiritual piety and competence. We are in over our heads, and things aren't looking very well from our perspective. There is only one thing to do—throw our hands into the air and cry out, "Pick me up, Daddy! I can't see from down here." (God's Eye View, p. 20)

SCRIPTURE READING
Luke 18:10–14, where Jesus compares the self-righteous and religiously correct prayers of a pompous Pharisee to the contrite prayer of a repentant tax collector, with a startling conclusion.

IT SEEMS THREE of the least politically correct topics among the churchgoing members of the "me generation" include messages dealing with reliance upon God, pride, and sin. I suspect God made these some of the most prominent subjects in the New Testament for a good reason.

Are you a child of the "lift yourself up by your own bootstraps" American culture? Or are you a public God addict with no inhibitions about your

God addiction? It takes courage to go against the public flow. (It takes the presence and power of the Holy Spirit to do it successfully.)

Have you ever tried to pray or praise God when you knew pride or sin was lurking in your heart where no one but God could see it? Did you find it difficult if not impossible to maintain the pretense?

Pride unrestrained may lead good people to do bad things under a covering veneer of religious good works. We should all know the ultimate wages of sin. The solemn warning in the book of Hebrews cannot be reconciled with open sin in God's people regardless of our respective theological opinions:

> For if we sin willfully after we have received the knowledge of the truth, there no longer remains a sacrifice for sins, but a certain fearful expectation of judgment, and fiery indignation which will devour the adversaries.[11]

Perhaps the worst thing we can do as followers of Christ is to offer Him praise or petitions while looking at another person in prideful judgment. On the other hand, the best thing we can do is forgive one another and lift up "holy hands to Him" without jealousy or strife in God's family.[12] It is the devil's worst nightmare.

> The process of waiting on God in persistent and passionate worship almost seems like work to us; but Satan sees it in far more dramatic terms. He *fears* and *dreads* the day God's people set their hearts to pray and worship the Most High God . . .
>
> The enemy is at ease knowing that we love religious formulas and fleshly equations so much. He doesn't even get especially upset when we begin to sing anointed songs by gifted psalmists and worship leaders . . . It's when passion is mixed into the recipe that the kingdom of darkness begins to fear the Light! (p. 21)

PRAYER

Lord, I'm finished with my do-it-yourself righteousness plans and revival schemes. All I know is that I'm desperate for You. Sometimes I'm not sure I know how to pray anymore, because You clearly cherish my addiction for You more than any achievements I claim to have apart from You. I will make no boast before You—all I know is that I need You, I want You, and I love You. My chief joy is to worship You and enter Your presence.

The Virtue of Zero

Less Is Better and Nothing Is Best

Sometimes it's better to bulldoze away the debris of collapse, failure, and destruction by fire and start over with nothing. Any thoughtful survey of the Scriptures supplies abundant proof that this is God's preferred route for redeeming fallen people and building His kingdom with them.

Welcome to the world as God sees it. We live in an upside-down realm where man's wisdom is really folly, and the best we have to offer Him will never be good enough—yet He loves us anyway. Thank God for the virtue of zero, where less is better and nothing is best.

Day 1

"Blessed Are the Zeros"

Tryouts for God's team are radically different from those for any other team in the universe. To begin with, no one is "good enough." We join out of our necessity to lean instead of our ability to leap. We are rated for our capacity to go low instead of our ability to go high.
(*God's Eye View*, p. 23)

SCRIPTURE READING

1 Corinthians 1:26–29, where we discover just how much God favors the foolish, the weak, the base, the despised, or even the unseen as "building materials" and subcontractors for establishing His kingdom in the midst of our upside-down world.

DO YOU BELIEVE GOD wants you to "become a loser for Christ"? God doesn't particularly prize stupidity, but He does honor honesty and humility. He doesn't ask us to pretend that we don't know how to think, plan, solve problems, or learn new concepts. We can do all these things, but no matter how well we do them, we will be no match for God—or for His divine assignments in our lives. They are, by definition, supernatural.

The Scriptures say, "For in Him [Jesus] dwells all the fullness of the Godhead bodily."[1] Watchman Nee, the Chinese church leader, author, and martyr, wrote a book about Him, titled *Christ: The Sum of All Spiritual Things*.[2] Perhaps we could borrow Brother Nee's title and say, "Blessed are the zeros, for they shall be filled with 'the Sum of all spiritual things.'"

The apostle Paul was, arguably, one of the greatest intellects of his era, yet he counted all his accomplishments but "rubbish" in comparison to the surpassing knowledge of Christ.[3] I doubt if any of us could claim to have accomplished as much as Paul did, but he did what he did by pursuing and leaning upon God with all of his being.

Does God have different "tryout" standards for college physics professors, brain surgeons, mechanical engineers, full-time mothers, or short-order cooks? No, the only way you will enter God's kingdom is to humble yourself and "become as a little child." He is more interested in the passion of your heart than in the procession of your credentials. The process of conforming to Christ's image continues and intensifies the longer you walk with Him.

> The highest positions on the God squad go to the least among
> us, and the places of great honor go to those who come to Him
> with the emptiest and hungriest hearts. This is the virtue of zero,
> and one of the secrets to attaining a God's eye view of life. (p. 23)

It seems that John the Beloved, the disciple who loved to lay his head on the Master's chest at mealtimes, just couldn't get enough of his Lord.[4] He wasn't any "weaker" than the other disciples—just hungrier. In the end, it was John who received the final revelation of Jesus Christ and the Father's end-time scenario.

What is the secret to the virtue of zero? It seems to be hunger for the presence of the Lord. Are you feeling hungry again? The Master is waiting . . .

PRAYER

Lord, it's me again. I'm not coming to You because You would be blessed by all my abilities, strengths, and accomplishments. I'm coming because I'm hungry for You. None of my abilities or gifts possess the power to draw me closer to You—only my hunger, passion, and love can do that.

I will reduce myself to zero every day if it means I can be closer to You; but I know You turn right around and build me up and exalt me in Your strength. If it is a contest of love, then winning is an impossibility; but "losing" to You is my greatest joy.

Day 2

Birthing the Miracle of Grace at Ground Zero

The unpleasant truth is that much of the work of character development takes place near what we might call our personal ground zero. Scientists coined this term around 1946 to describe the point at which a nuclear explosion occurs. I'm using the term to refer to "the center or origin of rapid, intense, or violent activity or change; the very beginning: square one."[5] More recently this term was used to refer to the place of devastation left after the tragedy of the Twin Towers of the World Trade Center in New York City. (God's Eye View, p. 24)

SCRIPTURE READING
2 Corinthians 12:9, where God describes the "grace at ground zero" principle of His kingdom.

HAVE YOU NOTICED in your pursuit of God that personal failure and desperation often cause God to draw near (while satisfaction in personal accomplishments or claims of personal holiness seem to repulse Him)?

God told the apostle Paul point-blank, "My grace is sufficient for you, for My strength is made perfect in weakness." Paul immediately added, "Therefore most gladly I will rather boast in my infirmities, that the power of Christ may rest upon me."[6] This is the "grace at ground zero" principle in one concise statement. Unfortunately, many Christians seem to overlook this passage in their study of God's Word. *Would you be willing to wait in line to hear a message or sermon about "boasting in your infirmities"?*

I've noticed that very little spiritual growth occurs during our stays on the mountaintops of life. Growth seems to explode, however, every time we struggle with sin or wrestle with God in the valleys and lowlands of human frailty. This is His way of birthing a miracle at the ground zero in our lives. Answer this "rhetorical" question: In your opinion, *is it easier for God to fill you with His presence when you are at "zero" or when you are "full of yourself"?*

> When Saul, the murdering religious fanatic, reached a *low* point on the Damascus road, it became the starting point for the high calling of his life. Thirty seconds in the manifest presence of God converted the murderer named Saul into the martyr named Paul. But he had to come to a personal ground zero. He referred to this "rapid change" the rest of his heroic life. Ground zero has the potential to birth heroes. (p. 25)

Have you been permanently changed by a "ground zero" in your life? Have you allowed God to birth heroic dreams and insatiable hunger for His presence through the pain and difficulty you've experienced in your life? If you yield to the Holy Spirit, He will elevate you to your high calling using life's low points as a launching pad.

PRAYER

Lord, I know You have given us powerful promises in Your Word concerning prosperity, victorious living, and divine health. I believe and receive every single promise You've made for us; yet my first response is to fall at Your feet in weakness, frailty, humility, and worship.

Every time I proclaim Your Word and stand on Your promises, I will think of You first and bow at Your feet as a living sacrifice. Thank You for every blessing from Your hand, but my greatest need is to look upon Your face and see Your glory.

God Loves the Challenge of a Zero Balance

God loves to start God-sized projects using "human zeros." He "gives life to the dead and calls those things which do not exist as though they did." You are chasing the God who kept His promises and delivered the Savior to the world through the infertile wombs of Sarah, Rebekah, and Rachel, the wives of the patriarchs in the Old Testament.[7] God even used the womb of a prostitute named Rahab from Jericho to carry on the lineage of the Messiah.[8] These are true stories of zeros turned heroes!

Finally He conceived the Messiah in the womb of a young virgin named Mary who was engaged to a carpenter named Joseph.[9] Our God loves the challenge of a zero balance. To us, they look null and void, but from His viewpoint they represent pregnant emptiness and untapped potential waiting for divine touch. (God's Eye View, p. 26)

SCRIPTURE READING
Exodus 4:10–14, where Moses puts his foot in his mouth and replies to God's divine assignment with the plea, "Why don't You send someone else?"

ARE YOU A "CHALLENGE" to God? Moses represented a major zero or possibly a negative balance on God's ledger. He was born a deliverer, raised and educated as a prince of Egypt, and banished from his own people and the house of Pharaoh as a murderer and traitor. Surely this man's mandate to lead had permanently expired! Yet God *anticipated* Moses' reluctance and arranged for Aaron's arrival ahead of time.[10]

Saul the Pharisee's significant academic, theological, and intellectual abilities represented a serious challenge to God's purpose for his life. It took an unforgettable thirty-second encounter with the presence of God to help him realize that his educational and religious credentials were not enough to carry him into God's purposes. He *chose* to remove his reliance on self and place it totally upon God, and the rest is history. *What will happen if you do the same? What will people remember about your life in the next generation?*

Paul's intelligence and in-depth rabbinic training still show up in his writings to the church, but God used them only after Saul the Pharisee laid himself on the altar of surrender to become Paul the servant of God. *Are there strengths and abilities that you need to lay on the altar of sacrifice right now?*

Many Christians face a different set of problems in their walks with God. They battle more with feelings of unworthiness and weakness than with proud thoughts of their personal abilities and tremendous value to God and the kingdom. *Have you disqualified yourself from service or leadership because you've taken up residence among the ash heaps of your personal ground zero?*

> If all you have to sow into God's ground is your weakness, your pitiful praise, or a tiny seed of faith, then your "zero" may be enough to birth a miracle in your life! God is waiting for us to run to Him when we wake up at ground zero. One of the greatest opportunities we have to give Him glory is *the day we discover we are helpless, hopeless, and worthless unless He shows up.* (pp. 28–29)

Saul the Pharisee didn't wait until his life was in shambles to turn to Jesus the Messiah, but it *did* take an encounter with the living God to change his mind first. How about you? *Will you make the choice now, or wait until God knocks you off your feet or until life's circumstances reduce you to a personal ground zero?* (The question still applies to you, even if you have already received Jesus Christ as Lord and Savior. He wants *all* of you *all of the time*, not just enough to write your name down in the Book of Life.)

PRAYER

Lord, I surrender all to You right now. I refuse to wait until my stubbornness leads You to knock me off my feet, and I'm not willing to delay until circumstances land me in a heap of ashes and broken dreams. I surrender to You now, without condition or limitation. My life is Yours to command. Be gloried in me as I live a life of unbroken worship before You.

Day 4

Don't Bury God's Investment in You!

Remember that preservation and planting are two entirely different processes. *God didn't save and deliver you so you could preserve His gift in a sealed jar and live life as usual. He expects you to* plant *your life, your gift, and your inadequacy in the soil of faith and die so He can live through you. He loves you, but He is also looking beyond you to the* harvest *He will produce* through you.

Don't bury the investment God has made in you, no matter how small it is. He is trying to use your emptiness to openly display His fullness. Never side with the father of lies and say, "Well, He's finished with me here." (God's Eye View, p. 30)

SCRIPTURE READING
Matthew 25:25, which illustrates the danger of burying God's investment in the soil of fear, timidity, and unbelief.

MOST OF US LIVE as if God invested His Son in humanity just to make a batch of canned preserves. *What would God find if He sampled the spiritual fruit in your church?* Would He find mostly jelly samples—the kind that are mostly sugar with very little substance or genuine fruit in the container? Would He end up with a jar of sour-faced, pickled saints?

The Lord planted Himself in the earth to make disciples who in turn would *make more disciples* who would live and minister just as He did. Unfortunately, many in the modern church seem to be more interested in preserving their boarding passes to glory than in pursuing the King of glory.

I remember reading somewhere, "If anyone desires to come after Me, let him deny himself, and take up his cross daily, and follow Me."[11]

People in other nations sometimes criticize Americans for their tendency to think that the entire world revolves around what is most important to America. It appears that many American Christians have a far more serious problem: *We sometimes act as if God exists solely to save, bless, and provide for us and lend His name to our grand accomplishments in this life.* The truth is that we exist to glorify, honor, and worship Him.[12]

God made a priceless investment in your life: How will you deal with it? *"But all I have to offer Him are my failures and weaknesses . . . What investment did He make in me?"* He invested *Himself* in you. Will you give yourself back to Him in response?

View everything else—your job, your abilities, your career track, your education—as accessories to a vehicle, as part of the means to a greater goal of following Christ.

Plant yourself in the soil of faith and become an uninhibited God Chaser. Allow God's investment in you to flower into supernatural bloom.

PRAYER

Lord Jesus, You gave Your life for me and loved me before I even knew You. The least I can do is give my life to You. I plant my life in Your hands, in Your faithfulness, and in Your kingdom. I long to hear You say, "Well done, good and faithful servant."

The Great Significance of Nothing

Nothing is far more significant to God than something. When you reach the point where you can't take any credit, you are standing in fertile ground for glory. This is the great significance of nothing.

Now for a shocking revelation: your vision, your ministry, and your circumstances must require a miracle, or God literally will diminish your resources until He gets you on miracle territory. (God's Eye View, p. 31)

SCRIPTURE READING

Psalm 127:1–4, where God makes it clear who must build His house, who guards the city, who blesses families with children, and who gets the glory for it.

FROM THE BEGINNING of time, people have offered to do something, make something, or give something to God that they value. Most of the time He has responded by giving them *His* preferred gifts or plans for the future—plans that seemed to start where their resources ended and His resources began. *Has this ever happened to you?*

- It happened to Moses, who thought he would deliver Israel with a fatal blow, but was sent back to the task armed only with a shepherd's rod and the glory of a personal encounter with God.[13]
- It also happened to Peter, who offered Jesus the strength of his strong will and clear leadership abilities, but was sent back to the task armed with a gentle reminder of his greatest failure and a triple exhortation to feed the Lord's sheep.[14]

It is better to seek the heart of God *first* and find out what He wants than to make blind assumptions and offer Him something He has never asked for.

What does this mean in practical terms? Could it mean we should structure our services around the one thing God the Father actively *seeks* in the earth (worship in spirit and in truth) rather than around those things that most minister to *us?*[15]

Has God asked you to do something you know you cannot do in your own strength? Praise and worship Him. You may be in line for a harvest of divine glory.

Are you facing circumstances for His name that absolutely require a miracle? Does it appear that everything will collapse unless God shows up? Rejoice! It appears that you have entered miracle territory. Worship Him until His presence comes (and watch what happens to the weight of circumstances on your shoulders).

PRAYER

Father, I don't know exactly what to do but my eyes are on You. From a lower perspective, things seem shaky right now. From the higher perspective in Your presence, everything is under control—Your control. Thank You for giving me peace that passes all earthbound understanding and a God's-eye view of my situation. The great significance of my "nothing" is that it gives me the perfect opportunity to put all my trust in You. I worship You, Lord, and find rest in Your presence.

Wait Until You're Weak; Wait Until He Renews Your Strength

We love miracles and dramatic testimonies of God's faithfulness, but we don't like the process He uses to dial down our resources until we get to the place of where only He can do it. We especially dislike the wait. And we don't relish the relinquishment of control. God's Word still says, "Those who wait on the LORD shall renew their strength,"[16] regardless of the way we feel. If you don't have enough strength, perhaps you haven't been a good waiter. (God's Eye View, pp. 39–40)

SCRIPTURE READING

1 Peter 5:5–6, where Peter warns us to humble ourselves or be humbled by God's resistance against us.

WHAT DOES HUMILITY have to do with "waiting"? It all depends on what you think waiting is. If you believe that the biblical term *waiting* only means "to wait around until something happens," then humility doesn't seem to be related to waiting at all. If you understand that "waiting on the Lord" also means "to serve and minister to the Lord," then humility is almost indivisible from the act of waiting.

Yes, all of you be submissive to one another, and be clothed with humility, for "God resists the proud, but gives grace to the humble." Therefore humble yourselves under the mighty hand of God, that He may exalt you in due time.[17]

You can't even approach God unless you are clothed in humility. In addition to that, it is difficult to *attract* God when you approach Him in your own strength, ability, and resources. I read somewhere that "the sacrifices of God are a broken spirit, a broken and a contrite heart—These, O God, You will not despise."[18] Divine appointments and holy encounters tend to occur at intersections of human weakness and Divine strength, and junctions of human emptiness and Divine fullness.

> The rugged territory between *having enough* and *not having enough* features the same geography as the place between the *already promised* and the *not yet received*. If it were up to us, we would choose the easier path and live on one side or the other. It isn't up to us.
>
> God put us in the middle on purpose. He carefully plants us in places of destiny where our pain, our faith, and our passion collide with His abundance, faithfulness, and compassion. Everything you've longed for is already promised and paid for in full, but perhaps it hasn't been delivered yet. Heaven's blood-certified check is in the mail. (p. 40)

Like it or not, it appears God puts us "in the middle" on purpose. Our destiny will only bloom in the pressure of adversity, difficulty, and desperation that moves us from the realm of our strength to the universe of His unending, immeasurable, and unmatched strength. Everything you've ever longed for is already promised . . . and His name is Jesus, the Son of God. Worship until He comes in a divine collision of crying need and abundant supply.

PRAYER

Lord, I feel as if I'm in the middle again. I don't do what I want to do, and I do the very things I don't want to do. All I know is that I want You, I want to be like You, I want to live, serve, and love others as You did—but I am weak and in need of Your mercy. My heart is broken over the countless ways I displease and fail You each day—please forgive me and lift me higher. Let me sit with You in Your strength and see with Your eyes, in Jesus' name.

Is Your Mountain Big Enough?

> *If your faith is too weak to accomplish your assigned task, it's probably because your mountain is not big enough! If you feel God has already brought your something to nothing and you still see nothing but failure ahead, take heart. An even greater destiny awaits you than you previously suspected. (God's Eye View, p. 40)*

SCRIPTURE READING
Matthew 17:20; 21:21–22, where on two different occasions Jesus says faith on the scale of a tiny mustard seed possesses all the power needed to remove a mountain. (He doesn't bother to specify the size of the mountain—I suppose that if you've moved one mountain, you can move another.)

IS YOUR MOUNTAIN BIG ENOUGH *to propel you into your destiny in Christ?* Abraham Lincoln is today one of America's most popular and respected former American presidents, but he seems to have lost as many political races as he won.

Lincoln failed to win reelection to his first state legislature position because he took a moral stand against what he felt was a politically motivated war against Mexico. Dejected, Lincoln left politics in 1848. It took the moral mountain of expanding slavery to propel him back into the political battle in 1854.

The difficult six-year road to the White House honed his abilities to refute opponents by skilled argument and persuade the nation with logic and strong appeals to the truths of God's Word. Lincoln would lead the nation through some of its darkest hours and help remove the ungodly mountain of slavery, but he wasn't really the man he was destined to be until he encountered a mountain too great for him to remove by himself.[19]

Do you suspect your life is following the pattern of Lazarus? You know the Savior of the world personally, yet you wonder if He is *ever* going to answer your call for help? One day goes by, then two. Everything seems dead and already buried. By the third day, the smell of decay is already defiling your fondest dreams . . . Surely it's too late now.

> God will wait until your dreams, your flesh, your ambition, and your ego are so dead that they stink! That is when He says, "Now is the time for a resurrection. It is *too late* for the hand of flesh to save and restore anything. No one else is going to get the glory but Me, for I am the only One who can do this." That, my friend, is the virtue of zero! Less of me equals more of Him. None of me equals all of Him! (p. 41)

Is your mountain big enough? Are your strengths and abilities dead enough to ignite a supernatural resurrection? It seems you are about to discover the virtue of zero and step into the light of divine provision once again.

PRAYER

Lord, I want to please You and fulfill my destiny in You more than life itself. If it takes an even bigger mountain and a deeper death to take me there, then so be it. I present my body—and my life—as a living sacrifice to You. Be glorified in my love, manifest Your strength and glory in my weakness. You are my First Love and Chief Joy.

No P.D.A.

Passion Police on Patrol

We must discard the foolish assumption that God has changed. He still regards passion and brokenhearted entreaty while shelving the unappetizing formalities of lukewarm religious pageantry. Victory is only one arrow of passion away. The crushing of our unseen enemies may depend upon the passion of our shouts of praise and our cries of dependence.[1] (*God's Eye View*, p. 53)

Day 1

Religious Refrigerants Endanger God's Environment

Sometimes people just decide that they have been called to join God's passion posse, the chosen frozen appointed and anointed to control and curtail any P.D.A.—public display of adoration—for Jesus that might make the cooler crowd feel uncomfortable.

These self-appointed and man-anointed religious refrigerants boldly seek every opportunity to stand before a public assembly of worshipers and say, "Cool down. We will tolerate absolutely no P.D.A. in this holy place." (God's Eye View, p. 45)

SCRIPTURE READING

Luke 19:40, where Jesus answers the passion police from the Pharisee precinct, "I tell you that if these should keep silent, the stones would immediately cry out."

SOME TIME AGO scientists discovered that certain refrigerants used in air-conditioning systems were especially dangerous to the ozone layer of our planet. National leaders took notice and passed legislation making it illegal to use or dispose of those refrigerants improperly. Automobile and air-conditioning equipment manufacturers were required to replace the harmful refrigerant in all new models with an environmentally friendly formula.

What is the condition of the worship environment in your local church body? In many congregations where the freedom of worship is less than best, any public passion shown toward God is quickly and firmly discouraged in the name of "not offending others." (Unfortunately, this clearly implies there is no problem with offending God, who specifically comes in search of passionate worship—He *hates* lukewarm things.)

43

It appears that religious refrigerants endanger God's environment in local churches, and He isn't very happy about it. In a very real sense, they are stealing His worship and quenching the Holy Spirit, who ultimately inspires and motivates worship in God's people.[2] *Have you ever participated in a passion police patrol during a church service or worship service?*

I suppose human coolants might be better tolerated if church were really about us, but the worship service in particular isn't. *Worship belongs solely to God.* The teaching, preaching, and personal ministry are blessed by-products that build up the members of the church, but they are *for us,* not for Him. Our *first function* is to *love and worship Him,* not simply to talk or preach about Him, as important as this is.[3]

> It is time for God Chasers everywhere to make a decision. When it comes to public displays of adoration for our God, we have important news for self-appointed passion police and every religious hall monitor lurking around the corners of a worship gathering: *we have a license, signed in blood. It certifies God's covenant and our commitment to fan the flames of our first love from now through eternity.* (pp. 45–46)

PRAYER

Father, I've made the decision and I declare it now: as for me and my house, we will serve, wait upon, love, passionately pursue, and fervently worship You. We acknowledge that we were created to worship and praise You, and we will fulfill our chief purpose as long as we have breath in this life, and for eternity in the next. We love and worship You, Lord.

God Sometimes Requires the Foolishness of Madmen

> *After Elisha took King Joash through the prophet's-hand-over-the-king's-hand process of shooting an arrow of the Lord's deliverance, he prophesied, "You must strike the Syrians at Aphek till you have destroyed them." (Notice that God spoke through the prophet before Elisha told the king, "Take the arrows.") . . .*
>
> *King Joash wasn't really listening to the prophet that day. He was too busy looking for something dramatic to happen. Miracles were common occurrences in the early ministries of Elisha and Elijah, and the king expected to see one on that day.*
>
> *The last thing Joash expected from his meeting with the dying prophet was a command that made him look foolish right in front of everyone. When Elisha told him to strike the Syrians until they were destroyed, he found it impossible to believe the total defeat of his enemies depended upon a ludicrous action more suited to a madman than a valiant man. (God's Eye View, pp. 48–49)*

SCRIPTURE READING

1 Corinthians 1:25, where we learn that the foolishness of God is wiser than men, and His "weakness" is stronger than men.

ONE OF THE REASONS many intellectual leaders have rejected the gospel of Christ over the centuries is the "foolishness factor." God deliberately uses foolish things to confound the wise. (He even uses apparently foolish people like me in the process.) His plan continues to work well.

How could God be "foolish" to people? Only the almighty God would invade our fallen world in the disguise of a helpless human baby and wait for thirty long human years before beginning the deliverance process. Only God would think of dying for His creations just to give them life again and restore them to His family—after they rejected Him and disobeyed His will.

The foolishness factor also accounts for the countless Christians who tell the Lord no when He gives them divine assignments. *Have you ever told God no because you couldn't understand why He would ask you to do such a foolish thing?*

People like King Joash have a problem with the apparent "foolishness" in many of God's assignments because they really don't believe God would make such embarrassing requests.

Do you somehow feel it is beneath God to dabble in the foolish? Remember that the apparent "foolishness of God" isn't foolish at all—it only looks that way to the one-dimensional spiritual perception of mankind. He is not the "God-in-a-box," He is the almighty God, who knows no limit or lack.

Perhaps the problem in many churches is that no one is really *waiting upon and listening* to God. We get too busy doing "the stuff" of church— we fill our days with an endless round of busy things that don't seem to impart life to very many people.

Life and history would have been much kinder to King Joash and Israel had he listened more closely to God's prophet. What might happen to us if we *listen closely* and wait upon Him next time we gather in His name?

PRAYER

Lord, I have no wish to be "valiant" in my own strength because I know it is useless as a tool to please You. However, I am willing to be a fool for You if my weakness allows me to receive Your strength and boldness. I will wait upon You and do as You ask, whether I appear to be a fool or a madman.

God Wants the Jewel of Obedient Passion, Not the Pearl of Public Approval

> *King Joash, if you had struck the ground five or six times, you would have struck Syria until it was totally destroyed. But you held your passion in check!*
>
> *You were* polite *instead of* passionate, *and you missed the moment of your greatest victory! You were more concerned with your dignity than with the will of Deity.*
>
> *Now you must live and die with the harvest from the seeds you have sown.* (*God's Eye View*, pp. 51–52)

SCRIPTURE READING

1 Samuel 15:22–23, where Samuel tells another disobedient king it is better to obey God than to disobey and make sacrifices afterward.

GOD DESIRES OBEDIENCE more than sacrificial religious apologies after deliberate disobedience. *The first command He asks of everyone is that we love Him with all our hearts, with all our souls, and with all our minds.*[4]

Jesus expected the twelve disciples to obey with zeal when He launched them on a supernatural mission to the Jewish people. He sent a dozen ordinary people out to do what no other band of people had ever done in the history of the world:

> Preach, saying, "The kingdom of heaven is at hand." Heal the sick, cleanse the lepers, raise the dead, cast out demons. Freely you have received, freely give.[5]

(Later, He said that these kinds of miracles should be *typical* among those who would believe in Him.[6])

To be honest with you, none of these descriptions or events come to mind when I think of the typical American church service. Passionless religious observance inspires descriptive words such as *restrained, respectable, predictable, lifeless,* and *remarkably unsupernatural.*

How could a "restrained, respectable, predictable, lifeless, unsupernatural" church be the empowered church *Jesus said would do* more *miraculous works than He did?* (He said, "He who believes in Me, the works that I do he will do also; and greater works than these he will do, because I go to My Father."[7])

Is it possible that many in our churches suffer from a modern version of the "King Joash Syndrome"?

> Somehow, between the grasping of the arrows and the striking of the ground, disbelief and the fear of man won the battle for the king's heart.
>
> By withholding his passion, King Joash foolishly sacrificed his nation's hope on the altar of public opinion and personal doubt. He would soon learn just how strongly his lack of passion in the unseen realm doomed his nation in the cruel realm of the seen. (p. 52)

The Lord told us to take up our cross *daily,* not just the day we repented and received Jesus Christ as Savior. He said that if we truly love Him, then we will keep His commands.[8]

Am I wrong, or is there is a "heat of passion" in the Lord's words that seems to be missing from the average Christian's life today? I don't remember even one command in the Scriptures that tells us to "cool down, calm down, and fit into the politically correct idea of church." (That seems dangerously similar to a description of lukewarm water to me.)

PRAYER

Father, I don't want to spend my life seeking public approval or the "easiest way" to do things. My desire is to walk and live in Your approval by doing things the "right way." I have no desire to cool down, calm down, or fit into some politically correct box—help me burn white-hot for You and obey Your commands each day of my life.

Day 4

Release Your Passion; Loose the Arrows of Prophetic Destiny

We are too quick to assume that God would never deal with us in the same way He dealt with King Joash. That is a dangerous assumption based more on lowered human expectation than on the eternal principles of God's Word. (God's Eye View, p. 52)

SCRIPTURE READING
Mark 10:13–16, where the disciples act as deputized passion police and try to stop the children who come to Jesus because they disturb the me-centered "big-people" service.

MANY CHRISTIANS HAVE a very unbiblical picture of Jesus as a mellow, laid-back, and nonconfrontational spiritual guru who always kept His passions at an even level. To make matters worse, they often model their lives after this passionless picture of their Redeemer—with predictable results. The Bible paints a totally different picture of the Savior of the world.

Jesus was the fulfillment of the prophetic phrase "Zeal for Your house has eaten me up,"[9] the day He physically overturned the money changers' tables in the temple. It is true that Jesus never *lost control* of His passions, yet His bold confrontations with the scribes and Pharisees provoked some of them to plot His death, and His love for people led Him to lay down His life on the cross. By any definition, Jesus was a *passionate* man. *How would you define your life?*[10]

All too often, we allow our destiny to be sabotaged by the passion police roaming the halls of worship . . .

If the people ever realize that they hold the arrows of prophetic destiny in their passionate praise and fervent worship, I suspect the sleepiness would vanish and apathy would give way to a thunderous display of passion. The enemies of God's people would scatter even faster than the shamefaced passion police as God Himself rushes to the scene of the act of passion to personally respond in kind. (p. 53)

The Word of God declares, "Let God arise, let His enemies be scattered."[11] *Do you want to see God arise in your home, in your church, and in your city or region?* Praise Him, worship Him. Build a tabernacle of praise for His habitation with your adoration.

PRAYER

Lord, I repent for all the times I held back my passion or compromised my convictions to calm the discomforts of people. You are my Audience of One, You are my First Love, and the only One I care to please. I release my passion for You right now as if it is an arrow in flight. Lift us into the heavenlies with You that we may pursue our divine destiny in Your kingdom.

Day 5

The Choking Church Requires Cosmic CPR

The church is choking on the larger-than-life servings of man-driven religion, and it is time to perform a heavenly Heimlich maneuver to dislodge the flesh blocking our inspiration. I pray God will perform cosmic CPR and impart the lifesaving breath of His presence to the fainting church.

Once we all come back to the dinner table again, things will have to change. Frankly I'm tired of talking about man. We need to talk about Him. He said, "I, if I be lifted up from the earth, will draw all men unto me."[12] (God's Eye View, pp. 57–58)

SCRIPTURE READING

Mark 7:6–8, where Jesus rebukes religious critics for focusing on the outward appearances common to man-centered religion instead of worshiping God in obedience to the Word and *from the heart.*

ACROSS NORTH AMERICA God sees millions of lips moving but far too little passion moving through human hearts to His. Praise of the lips without motivating praise from the heart is vain and hypocritical at best. The spiritual choking crisis is virtually universal—it happens in churches of every description, size, and condition. The cure is a divine encounter with the only true Object of all praise.

There was a man of the Pharisees named Nicodemus, a ruler of the Jews. This man came to Jesus by night and said to Him, "Rabbi, we know that You are a teacher come from

God; for no one can do these signs that You do unless God is with him."[13]

It seems that at least one Pharisee and elder of Israel among the many was a desperate man. Nicodemus was choking on the man-made system that was rejecting Jesus, and he risked the extreme disapproval of his peers to visit Jesus by night.

The next time we hear from Nicodemus, he is speaking up on behalf of Jesus in the face of his fellow Pharisees, and was honored to be cursed as a "Galilean" along with Jesus.[14]

In his third and final appearance in the Gospels, this desperate man demonstrates the passion of a soul beginning to be cleared of the fear of man. He dared to join Joseph of Arimathea and prepare Jesus' body for burial.[15]

What happened to this man? Nicodemus's encounter with Jesus initiated a gradual Heimlich maneuver of the spirit that was setting him free from religious bondage and the fear of man.

Are you "choking on larger-than-life servings of man-driven religion" that block your ability to praise and worship God freely? Ask God to force that blockage out of your life with an emergency procedure of the Holy Spirit. Your destiny could be at stake . . .

PRAYER

Lord, dislodge every fleshly obstruction blocking my inspiration from Your presence. Perform cosmic CPR if necessary to impart the lifesaving breath of Your presence to me, to my family, and to my church family. I've made up my mind to keep my eyes on You and pursue You on the winds of fervent praise and worship.

Day 6

Act Like You're Married and Loving It

> *For too long we've pulled back in fear every time we heard the "schoolmarm spirit" whispering to our assembly of worship, "No P.D.A.! No P.D.A.!" The sad truth is that the whole time we've had the license for passionate worship in our pockets. Jesus paid for it with His own blood.*
>
> *Nothing attracts God or disturbs complacency so well as passionate worship. (God's Eye View, pp. 58–59)*

SCRIPTURE READING
Ephesians 5:25–28, where the apostle Paul tells husbands to model their love toward their wives after the love and sacrifice Jesus Christ displayed for His bride, the church.

BEFORE YOU MOVE ON, take another look at Paul's words in Ephesians 5. He said in part, "He who loves his wife loves himself. For no one ever hated his own flesh, but nourishes and cherishes it, just as the Lord does the church." Now tell me honestly: *Do you really believe Jesus would be content to claim a coldhearted, self-absorbed, and passionless bride?*

Set aside all the distractions for a moment and consider all the things Jesus Christ has done for you and the church. When you think of Him, are you moved with passion or bored to tears?

> I feel passion welling up in me as I write these words. I'm doing my best to maintain my dignity, but you don't know what He's done for me this week! No one has any right to tell

me how passionate I can or cannot be about my Redeemer and Healer. (p. 60)

The humor, literature, and folk wisdom of our culture assume love grows cold when wrapped in the bonds of marriage. I believe love should burn hotter and stronger with every shared experience in a marriage. As believers and as Christ's body in the earth, we must learn how to act and live as though we're married to Him (as His bride) and loving it!

PRAYER

Lord, it is our turn—it is my turn—to love You as You have loved us. You gave Yourself for us; You nourished and cherished us in unconditional and unbroken love; You pray for us night and day as our Intercessor and Advocate. The least I can do is offer myself to You as a living sacrifice.

Make Mary's Choice: Become the Generation That Said Yes

The church is at a critical junction right now; a divine window in time has been opened. We choose our destiny by what we pedestalize and prioritize, and God wants us to choose between Him and our religious ideas about Him. (God's Eye View, p. 62)

SCRIPTURE READING
Luke 10:41–42, where Mary's choice to worship is praised and Martha is encouraged to lay aside her many worries and obsession with works to share Mary's choice.

EVERYTHING IN THIS LIFE comes down to choices. We construct the house of tomorrow with the choices we make today, and the choices we make at certain key times in God's timetable possess the power to affect the rest of our days on earth. These may include choices concerning marriage, choices concerning God's purposes, and choices made in response to a challenge from God.

> God is looking for people who will seize the arrows of opportunity and say, "If You said strike the ground, then we will obey although we don't know the way. All we know to do is to loose our passion for Your presence." (God's Eye View, p. 63)

We face a choice today—a choice that must be made by every member of God's family, one person at a time. Will we release our fear of men and loose our passion for Him?

This is our opportunity to overcome our complacency and make Mary's choice. It is time for us to drop every distraction and religious work to position ourselves at His feet. This is our chance to become the generation that said *yes*. Destiny awaits our decision. (*God's Eye View*, p. 63)

The only way we can become "the generation that said yes" is for each of us, and each of our families and local churches, to say yes. If we move away from the security of our pews, chairs, and living rooms to assume the Mary position of adoration at His feet, nothing will be impossible.

People who experience divine encounters with the presence of God are permanently changed. They begin to love more, dream bigger, dare more, and adopt the language of "yes" in their relationships with God.

PRAYER

Father, I've made my decision to pursue You at any cost. I'm beginning my pursuit with one word—yes. I love You, and long to please You, and my life is Yours to command. I choose You and Your kingdom first.

Discover the Power of Position

Sashaying into God's Presence

It always helps to *know* someone who works in upper management at the bank, in the company where you are interviewing for a job, or in the Internal Revenue Service office.

You know they can't or won't break the rules, but they may be able to use the influence of their position to pave the way for you in some way. Perhaps they gain you more favor, despite a spotty credit history; or they might provide a personal reference and reassurance that moves your name to the head of the list of job applicants. At the very least, they may ask for just a little extra grace or reassure you with their personal knowledge about the mercy, kindness, and genuine fairness of the official who will handle your case.

The best of all scenarios is for *you* to be the well-placed individual, especially when the Authority holding all the favor, grace, and the ultimate say in all things is God. This is the power of position.

"More Power to You, Kid"

> *If we ever hope to understand how God works in our lives and churches, then we must realize that although God is no respecter of persons, He is a respecter of position. It is one thing to make your petition with passion and persistence. It is another thing to make your petition from the right position.*
>
> *The simple truth is, there is more power in the word* Daddy *than in the word* Mister. (*God's Eye View*, p. 67)

SCRIPTURE READING
2 Corinthians 6:18, where God states His intention to adopt us as His sons and daughters and give us family privileges.

"ORDINARY" PEOPLE like stories about the children of people in powerful positions because they have a unique way of derailing the official "stuffiness" of high offices, royal decorum, and executive etiquette.

Have you seen the famous photograph of the late John Kennedy Jr. in the Oval Office at the White House? He was just a little boy peeking out from under the executive desk of the most powerful head of state in the world—his father, President John F. Kennedy.

I've heard it said that Tad Lincoln, the son of President Abraham Lincoln, often interrupted important cabinet meetings and ignored the disapproving glances of generals, admirals, cabinet members, and legislative leaders because he wanted to see his daddy. (Somehow, it seems fitting to me for a little boy to bypass and usurp the pompous line of credentialed and encrusted bureaucrats encircling his daddy.)

Bureaucratic types *still* have a difficult time with people who possess the power of position. The scribes and Pharisees of Jesus' day were driven to the limits of sanity when Jesus said He was the Son of God—and then proved it by working miracles.

> But I have a greater witness than John's; for the works which the Father has given Me to finish—the very works that I do—bear witness of Me, that the Father has sent Me.[1]

> If I had not done among them what no one else did, they would not be guilty of sin. But now they have seen these miracles, and yet they have hated both me and my Father.[2]

The passion police patrolling the aisles of our churches are still exasperated by anyone who claims to have a living and vital relationship with God. They shouldn't be. This power of position is available to *anyone* who dares to die to self and live for Him. The power comes in as we become more and more like Him. It was the power of position that transformed Peter the betrayer into Peter the preacher, whose inspired words harvested three thousand souls in the first church service in human history![3]

Is there any "power" providing practical proof of your privileged position with God? Do you know Him (and His Word) so well that you come to Him as "Daddy" as well as the Creator and Supreme Power of the universe? It should be changing and affecting things in the world around you.

PRAYER

Heavenly Father, I come to You acknowledging that You are the almighty God, the Holy One, who lives "in unapproachable light."[4] Yet I also come by faith in Jesus' name as one of Your children, crying "Abba, Daddy!"[5] Complete Your good work in me, conform me to the image of Your Son, Jesus, and make a power-filled light to my world so I may bring You glory.

Day 2

"My Door Is Always Open . . . for Worship"

In our earthbound daily schedules, we tend to neglect one of the most powerful gifts God has given us as our heavenly Father. His desire for our worship amounts to a permanently open door to the presence of God, and Jesus' sacrifice on the cross gave us an incredible power of position that can come no other way. (God's Eye View, p. 72)

SCRIPTURE READING
Galatians 4:7 and Romans 8:15–17, where we are declared the adopted sons and daughters of God and joint heirs of God through Christ.

THERE WAS ONCE a young thief who climbed a high, ivy-covered trellis to enter a second-story window in the home of a wealthy landowner. He was caught in the very act of thievery, but the owner had compassion on the fatherless boy and arranged to have all charges dropped.

His compassion ultimately led him to adopt the boy and give him full family privileges, including a key to the front door and full rights of inheritance as well. Yet time and again, the adopted son could be seen risking life and limb to enter his new home using the high trellis in good weather and bad.

Each time he was asked why he chose to enter through the second-story window instead of the front door, the adopted son admitted that his actions were rooted in the old habits and ways of his previous position. It took him many months to overcome the homeless habits of an orphan and thief and take up the privileges of a chosen son of the house.

Even then he was uncomfortable in the house—he felt more at home in the alleyways and roofless haunts of his former condition. After years of appearing only to receive meals, certain gifts, and occasionally the praise of his adopted father, the son finally realized the blessings of relationship he was missing, and he began to live as the son he was asked to be all along.

> In our immaturity, we are content to reluctantly enter our Father's presence for the briefest moment to deliver a quick peck on the cheek, a flash of raised hands in momentary praise, and a boisterous song in a church service. Then we say, "There, that ought to do You. See You next week." (p. 72)

Our heavenly Father wants to spend time with us, to share our lives with us. Yet, it appears that we get too busy and too involved with far less important things. We almost resent His delight in our moments of communion. As my daughter told me several years ago, "That's the problem with you daddies . . . you always want too much love" (p. 72). If we could only capture the truth that His door is always open to those who insert the key of divine adoption in Jesus' name.

PRAYER
Lord, I repent for seeking the gifts and blessings of Your hand more than the intimate fellowship of your face. You've called me and positioned me in heavenly places through the Spirit of adoption. Grant me the wisdom to seek Your face first, and seize the key of grace to dwell in Your holy place. You chose me and ransomed me first, now I choose You and pursue You with all my heart.

Day 3

We Are Blood Kin

When you sashay *into God's kitchen on a mission of celestial persuasion, He is sitting there at the table of worship (waiting on you in His omniscience, although you don't realize it at the time). When you begin to worship, from your point of view, your singing may be top-notch, or perhaps it is just below performance standards. From heaven's view, virtually everything you can do the angels can do better—except they are not His sons and daughters!* (God's Eye View, *p. 73)*

SCRIPTURE READING

1 John 3:1, in which John commands us to consider the kind of love that caused our Father in heaven to call us His children.

GOD CALLS US His children, but He is still all God, all the time. He knows all things, and the Scriptures specifically say that He knows what we need or hope to ask for long before we ask Him for it.[6]

He delights in every *sashay* and childlike way we demonstrate in His presence simply because we are His own. We should also realize He loves us even though He knows our every weakness, failure, and fault.

He knows how often and how hard we battle with secret plots, wrong motives, and bad attitudes. That is where the blood comes in. We are blood kin. The crimson tide of Jesus' cleansing blood *covers* us at our worst as long as we enter God's kitchen as His children with broken and contrite hearts. (p. 73)

God never winks at our sin and disobedience, but He is quick to forgive when we honestly repent and put it under the blood of Jesus. It is His blood that binds us together, cleanses us, and marks the boundary between the world and God's kingdom.

We are all one family inside the divine bloodline of Jesus Christ. It is His innocent blood that guarantees our entrance into God's presence as children and coheirs with Jesus.

PRAYER

Lord Jesus, thank You for every drop of blood that You shed for me and others like me. Your blood is thicker than sin, and its crimson flow is a river of life to me and all who come to You. It is a privilege to be covered, claimed, and protected by Your blood. Because of Your obedience and great love, Lord, we are blood kin.

Day 4

God Sometimes Says Yes to Spoiled Demands

> *What happens if we barge into God's kitchen with the demand,*
> *"Give me my allowance, Dad. I want my promised inheritance right*
> *now"? Demands have never gone over well with parents on earth or*
> *with our Father in heaven. (God's Eye View, p. 75)*

SCRIPTURE READING
Luke 15:11–24, where we see the Father's reaction to prodigal
sons, prodigal daughters, and prodigal church congregations.

THE "PRODIGAL SON" was one of those children who barged into his
father's "kitchen" and demanded his inheritance immediately. His father gave
him what he asked for . . . just as God often allows us to run headlong
toward our temporary or selfish wants instead of toward our eternal destiny.

Very little imagination is needed to figure out what happened next,
because Jesus painted a vivid picture of the prodigal's descending fortunes
leading to repentance and the dramatic reunion of father and son.

Many in the church, including entire congregations, have demanded
immediate blessings and a minimum level of maturity to satisfy their
flesh. God has allowed the church to continue its flight from home long
enough for the energy and anointing levels to be exhausted. The longing
for home and the Father's embrace grows along with the supernatural
hunger pangs.

A supernatural hunger is sweeping through the satisfied church today.
Somehow our empty religious forms and rituals aren't enough—the
hunger for God just continues to rage in us.

It is time for us to "come to ourselves" and rise up from the pigpen of mediocrity and spiritual coma to shake off the mud and cornhusks of our bondage. Daddy is waiting for us with the golden ring of His presence in hand. The real questions are, "Why go through all the pain produced by self-centered demands for the Father's blessings? Why not pursue His heart instead and receive the blessings of His hands as well?"

PRAYER

Lord, I have no desire to become a prodigal son. Why should I, when You have already made me Your child, given me an inheritance, and reserved a seat beside You in heavenly places? You are my inheritance, You are my wealth and my wonder.

Our Responsibility for Deity's Pleasure

> *He is our Source and our heavenly Father. We should never get*
> *irritated with His persistent focus on worship and worshipers. That*
> *is the "problem" with our Daddy—He always wants more love.*
>
> *The human capacity to give worship is vastly exceeded by Deity's*
> *capacity to receive it,* yet this is the responsibility that comes with
> the privileges and power of position. (*God's Eye View,* p. 79)

SCRIPTURE READING

Ephesians 3:20–21, where Paul describes God's unsurpassed ability to grant our requests but adds, "to Him be glory in the church
by Christ Jesus to all generations."

FOR CENTURIES, kings and queens in England have trained their children for the rigors of giving up their rights to private lives and private
pursuits for the good of their country. They are being trained to properly
handle the responsibilities that come with the privileges and power of
royalty in England (and Great Britain).

Observant Jews have taught their children the responsibilities of privilege
and power ever since God spoke to Abraham about His blessing and the destiny of Abraham's children. *Are you, as a Christian, prepared for the responsi-*
bility that comes with the privileges and power of divine adoption in Christ?

> It is not that we are so "good" at offering Him praise and
> worship, but there is something special about the divine mix
> of the power of our position as His children with the power of

our passion for His presence that helps satisfy God's desire for worship. (p. 80)

God looks to us for at least three important responsibilities linked to our privileged position in Christ:

1. Intimate and passionate worship from the heart by free choice[7]
2. Prayer that avails much in establishing His kingdom on earth as it is in heaven[8]
3. The offering of our bodies as living sacrifices to Him to do His will in the earth[9]

How are you doing in these areas? Is there something you need to do; are there priorities that should be shuffled to put Him and His kingdom first? Why not now?

PRAYER

Lord, I was born to be a worshiper and a determined God Chaser. You have blessed me beyond measure, yet I have a responsibility to become a living blessing to You and to the people You send into my life. You expect me to pray fervently by faith until Your kingdom comes on earth as it is in heaven. Most important of all, it is my privilege to offer You my body, soul, and spirit as a living sacrifice that is totally acceptable to You.

Day 6

Can You Say, "Daddy"?

As people walk through the store called life, they point out a need or want and begin to ask the Unknown God, "Mister, I need that. I need hope; I need help; I need healing in my marriage, God. I really don't know You, but I need this and that." What they really need is the ability to say, "Daddy." The power of position places their petition on a whole new level. (God's Eye View, p. 80)

SCRIPTURE READING
Luke 11:11–13, where Jesus describes the giving heart of our Father in heaven.

FROM DELIVERY TO DEATH, Americans are groomed to become the ultimate *consumers* of goods and services. Only rarely are we taught or encouraged to be givers or servers. *Which category do you believe is closest to the heart of God? Which group most dominates the average church congregation?*

Have you ever met someone who claims to be an atheist? Most of the atheists I've met go along untouched by God for months or years until a crisis provoked by accident, disease, or death knocks at the door of their lives. Suddenly they show up at God's door with a want list, even though they don't know His name or what He has done for them.

In a way, born-again Christians are even worse! They *do* know the basics about what Jesus did for them on the cross of Calvary, yet they constantly approach God with both fists filled with their checklists of wants and needs—and barely one or two words of thanksgiving and praise in their mouths.

How many times have you gone through a worship service barely tolerating hymns and spiritual songs? How often do you go through the motions of singing songs of praise and worship *as empty corporate performances* rather than as heartfelt hymns of praise and adoration?

Genuine praise and worship have become two of the lost arts in many of our meetings. *Have you settled instead for the programmed praise of passive spectators and the passionless worship of those whose hearts are elsewhere?* (It often becomes an outward "form of godliness" without the power.[10])

If we ever grasp the power of passionate praise and the wonder of true spiritual worship, our lives and our churches will never be the same. Be prepared for change to sweep through your life when you begin praying and worshiping God as a chosen son or daughter instead of as just another petitioner in "the outer court."

How do you tap into the favor and anointing God has promised His children? Can you say, "Daddy"?

PRAYER

Heavenly Father, Daddy God, my heart contains both reverent fear of Your majesty and power, and fervent passion for Your beauty and intimately personal love for me. The least I can do is come to You with a heart full of praise and a mouth full of words of praise, adoration, and worship.

Day 7

Stay Near the Only One Who Can Affect Your Destiny

> *Where is the prophetic generation that will look at those who ask*
> *for a fresh word from the Lord and say, "You stay right there; I'm*
> *going to the mountain to worship"? Sometimes we must separate*
> *and segment ourselves and pull ourselves away from the daily press*
> *of voices and conflicting priorities. Nearness to the Father some-*
> *times requires us to put some distance between us and the earthly.*
> *(God's Eye View, p. 81)*

SCRIPTURE READING

1 Peter 2:9, in which Peter the apostle describes our position, status, and calling as a chosen generation, a royal priesthood, a holy
nation, and a special people anointed to proclaim God's praises.

WE LIKE TO HEAR certain words applied to us: *chosen, royal, holy, special.*
Have you ever thought through the meanings and implications of those
words? What does it mean to be chosen? It means you have been selected
from among many and set apart from the rest for a different destiny or
purpose. *Are you still thrilled about being chosen?*

You are royal because you share the blood of the King of kings through
Jesus; you are holy because He is holy. To be holy is to be set apart from
the profane for sacred things. Is your life holy or profane?

Are you unique and peculiarly suited for fellowship with God? God
says you are—what does your life say about you to people outside
God's kingdom?

> Once you receive the power of position through the blood
> of the Cross, you will learn to leave behind the opinions of
> man. Why? You know your Father is the only One who can
> affect your destiny. (pp. 81–82)

At this writing, Christians in North America and in most Western nations rarely face persecution or physical danger because of their faith in Christ. We face different dangers including the seduction of wealth and comfort, and continual entanglement in the affairs of our overly busy lives.

One of the most dangerous traps we face is the "fear of man." Too many churches and individual Christians walk too close to the cliff of compromise by trying to please people more than God. Only God can affect your eternal destiny. *Please God and allow Him to deal with the momentary displeasure of men.*

We shouldn't be surprised if "nearness to the Father sometimes requires us to put some distance between us and the earthly" (p. 81).

PRAYER

Lord, I am in hot pursuit of Your presence. Deliver me from the fear of man and the entanglements of ever-changing human opinions. As I put You first in every area of my life, I trust You to make everything fall into proper place and order according to Your divine purpose. I am confident that everything else concerning me and those I love will work out if I stay near to You.

How to Make a Fool Out of the Devil

Tattletales Can't Come In

The truth has been known for two thousand years, but most people still live as if the lie is true and the liar rules. If actions speak louder than words, then many people—including many Christians—fear the power of the devil more than the power of God.

The truth is that God didn't even lift a finger against Lucifer the rebel in the beginning; He simply had His angels instantly remove him and his cohorts from heaven.

The truth is that Jesus Christ has already defeated Satan on his own ground. The devil has been condemned, his power and keys to hell confiscated, and he has been sentenced to an eternity in the lake of fire.

Satan's only weapon against Christians on earth is the power of the lie. The truth is that through the blood of Jesus Christ and the gift of repentance, we have the ability to make a fool out of the devil—and he can't do a thing about it.

Day 1

Who's the Fool Selling Sin on the Porch?

There is someone the Bible calls "your adversary" and "the accuser of our brethren, who accused them before our God day and night."[1] This tattletale of tattletales works at his job 24/7, and he has been perfecting his craft over multiple millennia. He is a liar and the father of lies, whose "native language" is untruth.[2] . . .

Satan knows the path to your Father's front porch because it used to be the home address for him and his gang of losers too. He doesn't live there anymore, though. (God's Eye View, p. 88)

SCRIPTURE READING
1 Peter 5:8; Revelation 12:10; John 8:44, where the Bible describes some of Satan's most notable "character flaws" and the heart of his desperate plans.

EVERY FOOL can mock a king or great man, but it takes God to make a fool of the arch adversary of our souls. The enemy of our souls is far wiser, more powerful, and more eternally evil than any mere man can ever know; *yet the Lord has given us the key to making a fool of the devil.*

I don't encourage you to openly mock or belittle the devil in your own strength—I'm not sure God is interested in protecting proud and self-confident men or women who are foolish enough to climb into a cage with a lion to prod him with a stick.

What do lions have to do with mocking the devil? When we openly mock this fallen angel who "walks about like a roaring lion, seeking whom he may devour,"[3] we have passed "through God's screen door" onto the enemy's territory. Satan is very capable of striking back when you step into his lair to provoke him. *Stay on the righteous side of God's front porch.*

However, you are free and encouraged to "beat him to God's door" with your instant prayers of repentance and thus "make a fool of the grand accuser."

What does this mean? It means the celestial tattletale is in the same predicament that Johnny Tattletale faced in my neighborhood. He doesn't have any family privileges anymore. It means that he's stuck outside the front screen door, the barrier designed to keep out pests, bugs, snakes, and *used sin* salesmen.

As for the back door, that is strictly reserved for family members in good standing with the Father of the house. The only thing he can do is to stand outside on the front porch of heaven and hope he can access the ear of God and accuse the brethren from the wrong side of the screen.

That sets up a great scenario for you and me to make a fool out of the devil! (pp. 88–89)

PRAYER

Father, thank You for giving us the keys of the kingdom in Jesus Christ. Thank You for giving me privileged access to Your presence and the forgiveness of sins through the blood of Jesus. When the adversary brings the list of my many sins and failures to Your door, You welcome me into Your presence with open arms and declare, "I see only the blood of the Lamb— there is no sin here."

Day 2

Welcome to the Heart of Worship—No Devil Allowed

*Despite all the efforts of hell and its chief tenant, your simple
prayers of repentance beat Satan's accusation to the Father's throne
every time. Even before the fallen angel could scratch on the front
door, your brief prayer of repentance reached God's ear faster than
the speed of light via heart-to-heart dispatch. (*God's Eye View*, p. 91)*

SCRIPTURE READING
1 John 1:7–9, where John tells us to walk in the light and allow
the blood of Jesus Christ to wash away our sins.

I SUSPECT THAT worship is far more powerful than any of us can know.
Its most important virtue is that it pleases God. He actively seeks out
people who worship Him in spirit and in truth.⁴ *The second virtue of worship to God is that it infuriates, embarrasses, and terrifies the devil.*

> Since you bear the family name, you have exclusive access
> to heaven through the back door of the blood of the Lamb.
> Jesus personally ripped the veil that used to divide imperfect
> people (that includes *all of us*) from our perfect God. Jesus did
> it so we could have instant access to divine forgiveness and
> grace. Worship allows you access to places where Satan is for-
> bidden to go. It takes you places the devil can never go. (p. 91)

Why does worship infuriate the devil so much? Perhaps it reminds him of
what he so foolishly lost through pride and rebellion. It embarrasses him

because the very fact that we have taken his place makes him look foolish time and again and there is nothing he can do about it.

Worship terrifies Satan because it reminds him that God alone is worthy of praise, and that he can never enter God's manifest presence again (he would be destroyed—no evil can stand or reside in His presence).

What will you do the next time you are ready to put Satan in his place and assume your rightful place beside the Lord in heavenly places?

PRAYER

Lord Jesus, thank You for giving us "instant access" to the heart of the Father through Your name and precious blood. Our words of repentance speed from our hearts to the Father's heart at the speed of divine hearing while the accuser is left outside and alone, separated from the presence of God.

Day 3

Business Is Down at Diabolical Accusation, Inc.

> *Do you know why there is no record? It isn't because I'm inno-*
> *cent—I'm clearly guilty. It is because when I repent, an angel takes*
> *an ancient quill pen, dips it in the red blood of Calvary, and erases*
> *or blots out the record. That is why you can make such a fool out of*
> *the devil.* (God's Eye View, p. 92)

SCRIPTURE READING

Isaiah 43:25; Revelation 1:18, where we discover heaven's habit of
blotting out our transgressions, and two of the biggest keys Jesus
carries around with Him in the heavenlies.

IN THE THOUSANDS of years before the Son of God raided Satan's head-
quarters and walked away with his keys on Easter morning, the devil's
endless accusations against the sons and daughters of Adam and Eve usually "stuck." The entire world was wrapped in spiritual darkness and under
the dominion of an arch rebel. Then God sent His Son, Jesus Christ.

> The accusation business just hasn't been the same since
> Jesus died and rose from the grave. (p. 92)

Business is down at Diabolical Accusation, Inc., and that is good. But
it isn't good enough. *Every single branch of Lucifer, Inc., should be out of business—so why isn't it?* They are still around because sin is still here, and too
few human beings know how to access the throne through the key of
Christ's blood and name.

John was transparently honest about sin in the Christian life. He said:

> If we say that we have no sin, we deceive ourselves, and the
> truth is not in us. If we confess our sins, He is faithful and just
> to forgive us our sins and to cleanse us from all unrighteousness.[5]

The matter of our of guilt isn't in question—we are all guilty. *The real issue is, who is your Advocate?* He simply took the blame upon Himself and removed it forever (and He is to blame—or praise—for bringing down the fortunes of Lucifer, Inc., and every subsidiary).

PRAYER

Father, I run to You in Jesus' name, openly confessing my sins and seeking forgiveness and covering in Jesus' shed blood. I'm covered, cleansed, claimed, and comforted in Your everlasting arms—right now at the moment of my cry. Thank You, Lord, for calling me Your child. Thank You for dismissing all Satan's charges as false accusations. I am found in You.[6]

Day 4

Outrun Satan's Accusations Every Time

> *Our Advocate, Jesus Christ, has the legal right to do something considered totally illegal in every human court of law. He doesn't argue against the evidence. He destroys the entire record—including the evidence—of our wrongdoing because he has already taken the punishment for our crime.* (God's Eye View, p. 93)

SCRIPTURE READING
Psalm 103:12; Hebrews 10:17–18, where God describes His unique amnesia triggered by the sight of Jesus' shed blood.

JESUS SHOULD BE the envy of every defense attorney in the history of the world. He has never lost a case—even though every single client openly confessed guilt before the courts of heaven and anyone else who wanted to listen in.

Was it unfair or unethical? Absolutely not, but that is where the judicial envy stops cold. Jesus took the place of His guilty clients. He was tried, convicted, and sentenced—and the sentence was carried out in full.

Why is it that your record of wrongs, sins, failures, and shortcomings doesn't even exist? He made your record His record and then cleansed it with His own blood.

> There is no record of your sin—it has been covered under the blood of Jesus Christ who paid the price for it all. The only problem is that Satan can remember your sins—and he can't do a thing about it. That makes him look like the biggest fool in the universe.

What allows you access to that kind of a position? How is it that you can enter through the back door while Satan is required to stand outside on the front porch to make his endless accusations? *The key to the family house is worship.* (p. 93)

What if Jesus hadn't come? What if Jesus had refused to take up His cross and die for your sins and mine? I'm sure that guilt would have destroyed us or our predecessors by now. At the very least, we would all die in our sins. Thank God, He did come and take our place. Now He calls us to come up higher and sit with Him to gain a new perspective.

If you worship the Lord and allow Him to lift you higher, He will remind you that every time of crisis is just another opportunity to run to your Father's back door and worship Him as a child of heavenly privilege. Above all, remember that your prayers of repentance will outrun Satan's accusations *every time.* (pp. 93–94)

PRAYER

Lord, every time I sin or fail You, I launch a plea from my heart confessing my sin and asking for Your forgiveness. I want to bless and worship You, not disappoint You. Through the blood of Jesus, my plea outruns Satan's bitter accusations every single time. Thank You for Your tender mercies, Lord.

Day 5

Stuck on the Porch with That "Sinking Feeling" Again

In one sense, Satan is a literal parable of the wages of sin. To the earthbound perspective of the human race, this fallen angel still appears larger than life. He promotes the myth that he has the same attributes as God with virtually unlimited knowledge, power, and resources. The truth is, he is literally the tattletale stuck on the porch with a lie in his mouth and a sinking feeling in his heart. (God's Eye View, p. 94)

SCRIPTURE READING

Luke 10:18–20; Romans 16:19–20; 2 Corinthians 11:14–16, where Jesus tells us He saw Satan "fall like lightning from heaven," and we learn that God will crush Satan under *our* feet, and that the devil and his crew like to wear angel costumes to fool the unwise.

LOOKS CAN BE deceiving. If outward evidence really mattered, then it would appear that Satan really has things going his way today. The truth is that Satan only succeeds when God's people fail to know and be the people God called them to be.

The second the church discovers her true heritage and stands up in Christ, the enemy is left out in the cold and darkness on the front porch, shielding his eyes from the light.

What happens when you come around? Is heavenly light released from God's deposit in your life, or do demonic influences draw closer because they are attracted to the empty void in your life?

The devil started high but ended low. He started out as an archangel at the throne, was demoted to prince of the air, ate dust, became Beelzebub (lord of the flies), and winds up in a bottomless pit. I would say that stock in Lucifer, Inc. is tending downward. (p. 94)

Put everything in a higher perspective by worshiping the King of kings and Lord of lords. Your worship will land you in God's presence and leave Satan and his bunch out on the porch with a lie in their mouths and that "old sinking feeling" in their dark hearts!

PRAYER

Lord, I'm not interested in simply talking with the devil on Your front porch—I want You. I'm not interested in Satan's lies, manipulations, or his latest exploits. I want to praise and worship You until Satan and his crew can't stand to be near me. My eyes and my heart are on You, Lord.

"Everything Looks Better from Here!"

> Lucifer forfeited his place as the worshiping, covering angel
> and was renamed Satan, which means "opponent" or "adversary."
> When those of us in the church begin to worship God and "cover"
> Him with glory and honor through praise and worship, we are
> doing collectively what Lucifer was created to do in heaven. (*God's
> Eye View*, p. 95)

SCRIPTURE READING
Isaiah 14:12–15; Ezekiel 28:12–18; and Psalm 100:4–5, in which
we see a partial portrait of Lucifer, the angel of light, and his terrible
fall; along with the "protocol of ascents" we follow as chosen
"replacements," bearing our blood-bought worship into the royal
throne room of God Himself.

SOMETIMES WE NEED to stand up to get a better perspective on a problem or situation. It seems there are three sides or views of what happened in God's celestial throne room when Lucifer was ejected from
God's presence. God provided a partial description of what happened
from His viewpoint.

His highest-ranking angel became defiled with a cancerous spot of
pride and ill-founded ambition, but this wasn't just any archangel. Lucifer
was the "covering cherub" who constantly surrounded God with praise
and worship.

God changed the "decor" of His chambers on resurrection morning,
and ever since, His chambers have been "covered" with *living trophies of
His only begotten Son's obedience.*

The praise and worship from Tommy Tenney's heart cover one microscopic portion of one corner, but God loves to hear the passion wrapped up in that croaking Louisiana twang. A little farther over, He hears the soaring worship of Jeannie Tenney, and He delights in the sound (most human hearers would like it *much* better).

The second view is Satan's, and it is one of the most bitter memories in his rebellious head. He can't escape it, and the pain it produces nearly defines the essence of hell itself. It drives and compels this fallen angel to hound and harass Christians 24/7 in an attempt to steal their worship and silence the painful sound of genuine praise and worship rising to the heavens and the place of his former estate.

The third view of God's habitation is *ours. Do you perceive the eternal value of your praise and worship to God? Do you understand how severely you exasperate the archenemy of God and the kingdom with your simple songs of praise and worship from the heart? Do you know the violent warfare your childlike praise provokes in the heavens?* It threatens to unravel everything the enemy has worked for.

> Worship takes you up! It lifts you up! It seats you beside your
> Father. Everything looks better from God's eye view! (p. 95)

PRAYER

Father, it is a privilege to praise and worship You. May my every waking moment include thoughts of and longings for You. The activities and thoughts of the evil one are of no interest to me except where wisdom advises it; but Your thoughts and ways are a different matter.

I stand in awe of You, and everything looks better when worship lifts me into Your presence. You are my grand Pursuit, my magnificent Obsession, my chief joy in life and beyond. Blessed be Your name forever. May Your children rise up in adoration and praise and may Your enemies fall down in dismay and horror. Praise and honor be to the King of glory!

Unthinkable: Sibling Assault in the Presence of God

Every hour of every day, children of the King step out on God's porch to do the unthinkable. Trapped in the depths of spiritual amnesia, forgetting the countless times they burst through the back door in search of their Father's forgiveness, these blood-washed and forgiven Christians step out on the porch to accuse their siblings and help the father of lies get his story across! (I'm not referring to church discipline, which is ordered by God and motivated by love.)

When you stand outside the door of grace to accuse a brother or sister, you are doing Satan's job for him. When you start saying, "God, did You see what so-and-so did?" you are trying to remind God of things that He says don't exist. We don't need any more discouragers; we need some encouragers. (God's Eye View, p. 96)

SCRIPTURE READING
Revelation 12:10–11, where we see the final end of the accuser of our brethren; and Luke 6:37, where Jesus bluntly and forcefully applies the law of sowing and reaping to every judgment and condemnation we make against other people.

DURING OUR MORE pessimistic days, most of us have probably wondered, "Has the church scene turned into one nightmarish soap opera episode entitled, 'Backbiters and Gossips Take Over the World'?" Much of the damage done to the reputation of the modern church has been done by tongues rather than by the black deeds of fallen church leaders. If one word describes the world's view of the church, in my opinion it might be *hypocrite.*

God knows which people are on His porch and why they are there. The moment we decide to speak against a brother or sister in Christ, we have stepped on the front porch in the company of the other accuser—and God is listening. I can't imagine a worse place for a child of God. Imagine the atmosphere you would share if you sat on God's porch swing with the enemy of your soul. (p. 99)

In retrospect, it doesn't take much imagination to figure out the atmosphere existing around Satan on God's "porch swing." We have all spent an unpleasant morning or evening enduring the divisive atmosphere of a worship service dominated by spirits of judgment, condemnation, and hypocritical sparring between spiritual siblings. The combatants would do well to remember:

Deity's answer to Peter's critical knock from the porch of accusation was swift and blunt. You are known by those with whom you associate. The moment Peter left Jesus to join Satan as a presumptuous accuser of Divinity, he took on Satan's name as well as his game. Peter ceased to act like a friend of God and took on a new reputation the moment he joined Satan's effort to stop Jesus' progression toward the cross. (p. 100)

Virtually all of us have slipped through the front door on occasion to join Satan on that porch swing—we just couldn't resist taking a potshot at Sister So-and-So—after all, she *deserved it so much!* The truth is that she didn't and we shouldn't have. The same blood that covers our sins covers hers, and by the same token, the same condemnation we heap on Sister So-and-So is coming our way.

It is far better to stay in the light with Jesus on the right side of heaven's gate than slip into the shadows on the front porch with the prince of darkness. Stay clean, repent, and worship the King of kings; and all will be well.

PRAYER

Lord, I repent for every word I've spoken in judgment or condemnation of others. I release them into Your forgiveness and ask that You bless them beyond measure. I regret ever leaving Your presence to enter a battle You never commanded or blessed. I want to be known by the company I keep, and my heart is in hot pursuit of You. By Your grace, I will be an encourager, not a discourager of the brethren.

The Principle of Magnification

Make Mountains into Molehills or Turn Men into Grasshoppers

The principle of magnification is virtually universal in scope. If you feed or "magnify" your body and neglect your soul, you will essentially become a well-fed and well-dressed outer shell transporting a spiritual vacuum from birth to eternity.

If you feed your mind all the available input on your disease, childhood fear, or compulsive addiction, your harvest is absolutely (and sadly) predictable.

If you feast on the bounty of the Lord's table—if you consume His Word, drink of His Spirit, and rest in His presence, your harvest will be holy communion, heavenly treasures, and divine promises delivered right on time in this life.

The choice is ultimately yours. You have the power in Christ to focus your vision and attention on Him and make your mountains into molehills. Or, you have the option to turn your eyes away from Him and focus on your fears. (Beware: you may find yourself transformed into a made-for-sorrow victim, a grasshopper on a crowded sidewalk in a world of angry giants.)

Day 1

You Minimize or Magnify Him by Your Focus of Worship

David the psalmist declared under the anointing of God, "Oh, magnify the LORD with me."[1] *He was referring to worship. If worship* magnifies, *then does its absence minimize? (God's Eye View, p. 103)*

SCRIPTURE READING
Matthew 15:7–9, where Jesus expresses the Father's opinion of people who claim to be God Chasers with their words but chase after other things with their hearts and deeds.

WORSHIP IS A FOUNTAIN of focus and attention that never "turns off." You worship or pay attention to something every waking moment—you fill your thoughts, your eyes, and your words with things all day long.

What receives the most worship in your life? Is it your job, your spouse, your children, your hobbies, your money, your problems, or your God?

> Have you ever wondered, *How do you magnify a God who is so big He already fills the whole universe?* How do you magnify the omnipresent God? How do you make the Creator of the universe bigger? The truth is that we really can't make Him any bigger than He already is—He "fills all in all."[2] (p. 103)

It is true that God already "fills all in all." However, there are billions of spaces—contended spiritual territory—that God does *not* fill. I'm speaking of human hearts. Even born-again Christians seem to have a bad habit of "reserving" or shutting off the secret recesses of their hearts from

God, much as you might secretly steer unexpected guests away from your secret messes and toward the cleaner and neater rooms of your house.

Are there places in your life that are "off-limits" to the Spirit of God? Do you secretly hope He stays out of the room labeled "My Past" or "My Sexuality"? Do you leave God "outside" when you enter the room with the computer and connect to the forbidden world you've created on the Internet?

Perhaps one way we magnify God is to fill *our secret places* with Him, and to fill our vision with glimpses of His glory and grace. We also magnify Him when we openly share His work in our lives with other people and shine the light of His glory into their secret places of pain.

Do you freely share the One you worship with other people, or are you too ashamed or afraid of rejection to talk about the Lord to your friends?

PRAYER

Lord, please forgive me for every time I've rejected You or placed You in a position below something else I've worshiped in my life. You alone laid down Your life that I might have life. No one and nothing else can claim first place in my heart. I will fill my heart, my eyes, and my thoughts with visions of You and Your kingdom. I know that if I seek You first and put Your kingdom first in my life—if I magnify You with my worship—then everything else that I need will be supplied.

Day 2

Magnify Him in Wide-Eyed Wonder

When you look through a magnifying glass at a grasshopper, you are not making the grasshopper bigger; you are just making it appear bigger. The process of worship does not make God bigger; it just makes Him appear bigger. (God's Eye View, p. 104)

SCRIPTURE READING

Luke 24:13–32, where a single encounter with Jesus transports two disciples on the road to Emmaus to a state of wide-eyed, burning-heart wonder over His glory.

MY LITTLE GIRLS aren't little anymore, but I have hundreds of "snapshots" in my Daddy's Memory Book that permanently record those heart-melting moments when my little girls' eyes grew wide with wonder. It happened almost every time one of them saw a little puppy or touched a newborn baby. And every time, this proud daddy almost had a love meltdown.

God wants us to regain the wide-eyed wonder of our childhood in His presence. *How long has it been since His presence transported you back to a state of wide-eyed wonder?*

Unlike the grasshopper, God is already bigger than all created beings, form, and matter; yet the magnification of worship makes Him larger in *your* view. Suddenly everything about Him gets bigger in your eyes. That means His capabilities get bigger, His power gets bigger, and the force of all of His promises and wonder is suddenly enlarged when you magnify the Lord. (p. 104)

The three closest earthly companions of Jesus thought they had a handle on their great teacher and miracle worker. They had lived with and served Him for some time when He asked them to join Him for a climb up a mountain. They weren't prepared for the visitation by two of the greatest leaders in Judaism, but they "adjusted" by offering to build three shelters of honor for Jesus and His two distinguished guests.

Since they didn't "get it," the heavenly Father made an abrupt course correction and *magnified His own Son*. Suddenly the dignitaries of past visitations faded from view and Jesus alone filled their vision. *Are you trying to force Jesus Christ to "share a condo" with some other "past dignitary" or small-time god in your life?*

PRAYER

Lord, open my eyes to see You with wide-eyed wonder once again as a little child. You are the almighty God all the time, but I want You to be magnified in my life right now. Help me to see Your glory so my life will be forever changed on the earth. I set aside everything that I've tried to set in first place in my life, and I reject everything I once gave the status of a small-time god in my life. I serve one God and one God only. Be magnified in my life, Lord.

"I'm God's Postcard: See Anything That Can Help?"

Why does the world have such a skewed view of God? One of the most important reasons is that we have not magnified God in the sight of the unsaved. They look at our misrepresentations (and underrepresentation) of Him and His kingdom and say, "Nothing we see there can help us. Those people are as messed up as we are."
(*God's Eye View*, p. 104)

SCRIPTURE READING
Matthew 5:14–16, where Jesus commands us to shine and not hide so that our good works will cause other people to glorify or magnify God.

"SKEWED VIEW" may well be the most accurate way to describe the cockeyed way most North Americans see God through the church. If God is known by the company He keeps then God's reputation must be suffering a serious decline at the moment.

Most of His churchgoing companions seem to major on religious hypocrisy, stuffy and lifeless tradition, and a very unfriendly "inner clique" of the religious elite. *If you are "God's postcard" to your unsaved friends, how do they view the God you portray in your life?*

We must restore the principle of magnification. How do we do that? Worship magnifies God to the world. When they see and hear us praise God for His mighty works and His godly attributes, they begin to realize there is more to Him than meets the eye. (p. 104)

Is your life a song of praise and worship that magnifies God in the eyes of your friends, or is it a plaintive lament that makes them want to run and hide in discouragement and dismay?

PRAYER

Lord, help me to become a divinely appointed "postcard" of joy, love, and power sent from Your presence into their lives. Make me a carrier of Your presence and glory to transport Your light into every man's darkness and sorrow. May they read my life and see You in every word and expression of my daily life. Be magnified in me, Lord.

Day 4

Your Life Is a Window and a Magnifying Glass

> *God revealed Himself to the son of a moon worshiper and gave him a God-sized promise. Abraham used the rest of his life as a magnifying glass to declare and reaffirm God's power and ability to keep His impossible promise. Countless individuals, tribes, and people groups saw their first glimpse of God through Abraham's worship and faith in God. In the end, God's promise that all nations would be blessed through Abraham came true through Jesus Christ. (God's Eye View, p. 105)*

SCRIPTURE READING
2 Thessalonians 1:10–12, where Paul speaks of a day the Lord will come to be glorified in us.

IT APPEARS your life is a window into the kingdom of God. Is the view of the presence of God through your life cloudy, dim, and distorted, or clear and bright? Do you suppose it has much to do with *your own view* of God? *Does your proximity to His presence affect the clarity and nearness of your view of God?*

> Abraham's life illustrates how faith operates according to the magnification principle. He constantly magnified God's ability to keep His word despite facing years of contrary circumstances. (p. 105)

It is impossible to live the Christian life without faith, and it is impossible to please God apart from it. *Is your view of God based purely on the* latest experience you've had with Him, or is it also founded and rooted upon faith in His Word and His character as God? (*Hint:* Does your view of God *change* when circumstances change, or does it remain as unchanging as His Word on the matter?)

Put yourself in the place of someone who does not know God. Now ask yourself: *Would I be more impressed with the God who shows up in a person's hard times, or with a God who only seems to show up in the good times?*

Your life must magnify Him *all* the time, in good times and in bad. Then you will become a "Technicolor window" into the faithfulness of God *all* the time, in every season of life.

PRAYER

Lord, I yield to the work of the Holy Spirit, who urges me on both to want to and to actually do Your perfect will. Make me a transparent window, revealing Your unending faithfulness in my life. I long to be a magnifying glass openly displaying Your mercy, grace, and tender Father's love to all who look for You. Grant me the grace and faith to become a living witness to Your faithfulness in times of trial, adversity, and weakness. May You be glorified in all things concerning me.

Day 5

"That Thing I Greatly Feared Is Feared No Longer"

Faith and fear operate on the same principle. The alarming thing about it is that North Americans have allowed fear to so infiltrate our version of the English language that we have adopted "fearful language" as a matter of habit. How many times have you asked someone how he is feeling only to hear him say, "I'm afraid I'm catching a cold"?

Job said, "The thing I greatly feared has come upon me, and what I dreaded has happened to me."³ Have we made that our cultural slogan? (God's Eye View, p. 105)

SCRIPTURE READING

Matthew 12:34–37, where Jesus warns that we are justified or condemned by our words, and that in the day of judgment, we must give account for *every idle word* we speak.

"You're going to break your neck, Junior."

"That thing scares me to death."

"You're going to give me a heart attack some day!"

"I'm going to finish this thing if it kills me."

"You make me sick."

HOW MANY OF these self-pronounced curses have we spoken into existence over ourselves and our loved ones in the last month? The "modern sophisticate" in us wants to scoff at the idea that "mere words" may affect a human life, but God apparently disagrees with the sophisticates and places eternal weight on our words. He keeps a detailed record of *every word* we speak. *What have you been saying? Which way is your faith working—to lift you up or pull you down?*

> Focus on the size of your God, not the size of your problems. Joshua and Caleb focused their eyes on faith and the size of their God instead of the size of their problems. Decide for yourself which one you will look at, but you should realize that God is more than 432 times bigger than your biggest problem. He fills the universe and more. No matter how big your problem appears to be at the moment, your God is bigger still. (pp. 108–9)

Another young man named David managed to focus his eyes on the God he had discovered in the sheep pastures rather than on the giant standing in front of him, challenging the entire Israelite army.

At times it seems the church somewhat resembles the picture of the entire Israelite army shaking in fear-induced paralysis on one side of a valley while a pagan giant shouts threats and insults at them and belittles their God.

Where are the Joshuas, Calebs, and Davids of our generation? *Who will dare to take a stand based on God's Word and their intimate relationship with God?* He is looking for a people willing to destroy the works of the mouthy upstart from hell, a people armed with the intimate confidence they have in their Savior and Lord. *Do you have your God Chaser's worship sling and shepherd's staff ready for His call?*

PRAYER

Father, I'm pulling my eyes away from my problems, and I am turning my ears away from the scoffers and the "gloom and doomers."

It is time to fasten my eyes on You, Lord. This is the season to read,

---

meditate, memorize, and declare Your unchanging Word over my ever-changing circumstances.

I don't need a public opinion poll to decide my course—I have a much more dependable and everlasting Source of counsel and direction. That thing I feared, that uncertainty I dreaded, no longer holds power over me. I'm in hot pursuit after You and Your heaven's-eye view.

Worship Your Mountains into Molehills

When you fly high, whatever is beneath you appears smaller, and whatever you get close to appears bigger in your sight.

What does all of this have to do with worship? Worship is the spiritual equivalent of the power of magnification. Magnification possesses the power to turn mountains into molehills or men into grasshoppers. (*God's Eye View*, pp. 110–11)

SCRIPTURE READING
Isaiah 40:3–5, where the prophet prophesies of the One before whom every mountain would be made into a "molehill" and every valley "lifted up."

THINGS IN GOD'S REALM aren't as they seem in our world. And the obstacles and difficulties of this life have no power to influence or change the eternal realities of God's kingdom. However, God is well able to influence, change, intervene, or re-create things in this world to conform them to realities in His realm. *Your worship is the key to His willingness to lift you higher for a God's-eye view in times of trouble or concern.*

The Scriptures are filled with references to God's willing and eager response when human hearts cry out to Him and express their hunger and need for His presence. When we *worship* Him, He lifts us back over the fence into *His yard* and lets us see things from His elevated perspective. (p. 115)

There are some things that we all must endure and experience, even if we are the world's most experienced and successful God Chasers and worshipers. We must enter this world through a woman's womb (even the Son of God experienced this traumatic passage); we must experience the pain of loss (it happens if ever we become attached to family members, friends, or even a cherished pet); and if the Lord tarries, we must experience death. If God will not help us avoid these challenges, He promises to walk through them with us. *Would you rather worship or wring your hands in times of difficulty and stress?*

> Worship is the wind beneath our wings that lifts us up above the earthly realm. The truth is that if you are "in Him," then there is a place in worship to which you may go and sit with Him on high, and *look down* on the lesser issues below. I call it getting a God's eye view of life's circumstances. I know we often speak of getting a bird's-eye view, but wouldn't you prefer to get a God's eye view of the things that concern you? (p. 112)

If you worship Him, He will fill your vision and heart with His fullness, joy, and strength, while pushing away every competing thought about the size, fear, and threatening appearance of your life challenges. *Will you lay aside everything else to do what Mary of Bethany did when death visited her home? Worship Him.*

PRAYER

Lord, it is one thing to talk about worshiping You in times of ease and low stress. It is another to actually worship You when the weight of loss, the fear of death, or the terror of sickness and plague knock at the door of our lives. Even so, I will worship You with all my heart, all my soul, all my strength, and all my mind. Lift me on the wings of worship so that I might see things from Your eternal perspective and rejoice.

Day 7

Put on Your Game Cleats and Worship Him

Testimonies are birthed in tests that stretch you beyond your strength and resources. Miracles are born out of impossible circumstances where only God's strength and power will do. All of these things are possible and even probable in the lives of those who have learned that worship is not connected to circumstances. (God's Eye View, pp. 117–18)

SCRIPTURE READING

2 Kings 6:15–17, where the prophet Elisha's servant receives a vision adjustment and looks past the problems covering the mountain to see God's angelic solution looming over them all.

SOME OF THE BEST TIMES in my life with Christ were those moments when I said, "Lord, if You don't show up, I'm in deep trouble." The Lord loves to see how we react when we reach the end of our resources and native strength. *Will we cry out and curse Him, or will we cry out and worship Him?*

Spread your wings of worship and fly over life's circumstances. If you've run out of strength, then wait (and worship) a little longer!

The process of worship takes you higher than anyplace you have ever been. Throw out your padded spectator seats, and put on your game cleats. *Worship is not a spectator sport.* God is about to set you free. This is your moment—rise above the pain; you'll never be the same. *Wait* upon Him with your worship, and rise above the circumstances. (p. 118)

The world cannot be won or changed from a padded pew. Discard your spectator sneakers and put on your "game cleats." We must win the war on our knees in prayer, on our faces in submission and holy hunger, and on our feet serving others, meeting needs, and carrying the gospel to the hungry of heart.

"I know, but that pew is so comfortable, and all that other stuff makes my knees hurt."

> Is the Spirit of God stirring your heart right now? Is the tide of worship rising in your life? This is just the beginning. Only God knows where your *yes* to His proposal of worship will take you.
>
> . . . Will you magnify Him and turn your mountains into molehills or magnify men and live life like a grasshopper? (p. 119)

Let me repeat something for divine emphasis: *this is just the beginning. Only God knows where your yes to His proposal of worship will take you.*

PRAYER

Lord, You have been stirring my heart for a long time now. I've sensed that holy nudge to dig deeper into Your Word and stay longer on my knees in prayer. My soul reverberates with the possibilities of worship, of tapping into the eternal well of intimate communion with You. I say, "Yes," Lord. I will worship You with all my heart, mind, and strength. Lift me up where I belong, seated in heavenly places with You.

Reclaiming Worship
The Greatest Mood-Altering Drug

I suspect there are millions of people in industrialized nations who make regular trips to their local pharmacy to purchase one of many mood-altering drugs to make their lives seem to be something less than hell on earth. (And then there are those who don't use a pharmacy—they purchase illegal drugs to accomplish the same thing, but without a prescription.)

God has a better idea, and it begins with a divine appointment with the Great Physician. The guaranteed improvement in quality and abundance of life is maintained with liberal and regular doses of the world's greatest mood-altering drug—worship.

Day 1

Where Is the Worship?

> *If you read the book of Job, you will notice that the* first thing *Satan touched was not Job's children. The first thing he took was the livestock (including cattle [or oxen] and sheep). In the culture of the Old Testament, Satan had destroyed Job's ability to worship when he took away the man's herds of sacrificial animals. Only after he took away Job's ability to worship was Satan able to touch anything else in his life. (God's Eye View, p. 121)*

SCRIPTURE READING

Matthew 4:8–10, where Satan even tries to steal worship from Jesus Christ and redirect it to himself. (It didn't work.)

THE DEVIL IS a compulsive thief and liar, and his favorite target is worship. He doesn't steal for love, nor does he steal for greed (although he would if he could). He steals for revenge and is motivated by hatred.

Lucifer was *created* to worship God, but tried to steal it for himself. He separated himself from the purpose for which he was made—and he hates anyone who does what he can no longer do—worship God.

Take a moment to inventory your life. Begin by examining the way you spend your time, and compare those notes with your priorities in life (if you have written them down). *Is God first on your list and in your life? Do you spend more time worshiping Him than you do watching TV news programs or mowing your lawn? Is there a thief in your life?*

> Worship is the jugular vein of life in God's kingdom. *If Satan can stop your worship, then he will have access to anything else in*

113

your life. If you read the very last chapter of Job, you will notice that an interesting thing happened. (p. 121)

Is Satan wreaking havoc in some area of your life, in your family, or in your local church? Does he seem to be almost impervious to all the usual weapons of spiritual warfare? *Has Satan stolen your worship?*

If he has, then he has deprived you of your key to intimacy with Divinity. Jesus Christ is the Door, but your worship is the perfume and sweet offerings you bring to God to express your love for Him.

Change direction and force the issue right now. Begin to worship God, no matter what your circumstances look like.

PRAYER

Lord, You are my salvation, my hope, my song, and my chief desire. There is no God besides You, and my heart and life belong to You alone. Jesus, You purchased me with Your blood and redeemed me from death. My life is no longer my own, but Yours. I run to You with repentance in one hand and praise and worship in the other. My todays and my tomorrows are safely in Your hands. Blessed be Your name forever!

Continually Living on the Edge of Worship

> *God Chasers who live in the real world filled with conflicting pri-*
> *orities and obligations often ask me how to balance God Chasing*
> *with kid chasing, job racing, and spouse-embracing obligations. I*
> *understand because I must constantly balance my pursuit of Him*
> *with daily ministry obligations, an extensive travel schedule, and*
> *my vital relationships with my wife and three daughters. (God's Eye*
> *View, p. 122)*

SCRIPTURE READING

Genesis 18:17–19, where God explains that Abraham was trust-
worthy, in part because he knew how to balance his obligations
as father and husband with his greater call to be the father of a
great nation.

LAREDO, TEXAS, and its sister city, Nuevo (New) Laredo, of Mexico, are
unique cities because they both border on a river that divides two totally
different nations with different languages, cultures, monetary systems,
governments, and legal statutes.

Residents from each side of the river swap sides regularly en route to
their jobs, doctors' appointments, church events, and countless other
activities. Yet all of them know where to find "home" at the end of the
day—they are used to living on the edge of "another life."

You live in the world just as I do, but actually we live at the edge of our
native home, a spiritual kingdom just across the river boundary of the
blood of Jesus. *Do you know your way home on the path of worship?*

Here is my affirmation: I've made up my mind that even when I get pulled away from His presence by temporary earthly priorities, I am going to stay close to the door so I can slip back in at any point!

Some people find it easier to enter God's presence than others *because they never sleep far from the door*. They literally stay on the edge of worship. (p. 123)

What does it take to remain "close to the door" of God's presence? Have you mastered the skill of living in the world without being "of" the world?

Sometimes we allow our magnifying glass of worship to be stolen from us because we unknowingly set our affections and loyalties on the *wrong source*. It usually happens innocently enough, but the fruit of these misplaced affections can be very dangerous . . .

Never look at someone on a platform or before a speaker's lectern and say he is the "source of power." The person may be an *outlet* of power, but you could say the same thing about a twenty-five-cent wall outlet or a two-dollar extension cord from a discount store. (pp. 123–24)

These passages reveal at least two ways to misplace your "worship magnifying glass." The first applies to virtually anything that *attracts* you, and it rarely applies to anything innately evil. It is often your favorite TV show, hobby, sports team, or your career. The second way is to fall in love with God's "messengers" instead of the God who sent and inspired them.

Are you keeping your affection for God pure and white-hot? Are you putting your hunger and love for Him first, even above the love you should rightly have for a spouse or your other family members?

PRAYER

Lord, draw me near Your passionate heart that I may catch fire and bring Your light to everyone I meet. I repent for even the smallest of mistakes when I put my affection for people or things above my love for You. You are my First Love. Help me live and display Your love and light as if I had just crossed over from Your presence into the earth with shining glory illuminating my face.

Day 3

Don't Say You're Finished Before God Does

Discouragement is another diabolical key that opens the door for the thief to steal our goods. Perhaps you have awakened to a new day but felt just as bad as you did yesterday. In a moment of weary resignation and discouragement, you opened your mouth and released the fear that was in your heart: "He's finished with me here. I give up."

I feel the anointing of God to tell you right now, you will not fail, and I have witnesses to prove it: Samson and Moses. *Pick up where you left off! Restart your worship—reclaim your destiny!* (God's Eye View, p. 127)

SCRIPTURE READING
Psalm 34:18–19, where the psalmist assures us God is *near* the brokenhearted, and saves those with a contrite or crushed spirit.

THE COMMENTS SEEM to come automatically with every new challenge human beings decide to accept: "I can't do it. I look stupid—I know I do. This will never work. I wish I had never agreed to start this thing . . . It's *your* fault."

Think of your first fumbling attempts to ride a bicycle, to glide on ice skates, to type without looking at the keyboard, or to play basketball or hit a baseball for the first time. Our ineptness seems staggering and overshadowing at times, but God sees the big picture. He knows that all we need is a God's-eye view of the situation. *Are you fumbling, falling, stumbling, or missing the mark somewhere in your life at the moment? Are you ready to quit an assignment God gave you to do? Don't. Worship Him instead.*

God said, "Don't say you're finished with something before I am finished with it. Now go back to the same place where you just witnessed a miracle if you want another one."[1] Don't be surprised if God tells you to go right back to the last place you had a divine encounter . . . The moral of the story is this: *don't say you are finished before God does.* (p. 128)

Never, ever forget that you are not in this thing *alone.* God is with you every step of the way, whether you "feel" Him or not. I am a determined God Chaser and I love to feel the joy of His presence, but I learned long ago that He never leaves or forsakes me. That means you cannot fail in Him, no matter how many times you fall, fail, falter, or fumble things. The key is to put Him first in everything all the time.

PRAYER

Lord, how many times have I tried to quit something over the last five years? I've lost count, but I can tell You how many times You have "quit" on me—zero, never, not at all. As long as You stay with me, I will keep on dreaming, believing, climbing, overcoming, and getting up again. Even my failures and fumbles bring me gain—just another occasion to find comfort and joy unspeakable in Your everlasting arms. I love You, Lord.

Day 4

"Remember That It Belongs to Me"

> *Once I said, "Okay, I quit," He said,* It's about time. I've been trying to get you to that point for some time. Now I'm not going to let you quit. Pick it up again, but just realize it is Mine. (*God's Eye View,* p. 129)

SCRIPTURE READING
John 15:4–5, where Jesus warns us that apart from Him we can do nothing.

NO ONE WANTS to hear it said, but there are times when desperation, frustration, and outright failure become our teachers and counselors. God uses virtually everything in our lives to draw us to Himself. Those of us gifted with especially hard heads and stubborn wills often find ourselves in the office labeled "Office of Hard Knocks and Attitude Adjustment."

Have you been working at something in your life or ministry only to reap a harvest of growing frustration and a sense of total failure? It may be time to take it to the altar and give it up. If God gives it back to you, then He just took care of your biggest problem (you). If He doesn't, then it wasn't part of His plan anyway. Walk away and count your blessings.

> God is tired of arm wrestling us for His church, so He'll let us get to the point of desperation where we will just resign and say, "It's Yours, Lord. It is all Yours." That is when He will say, "Good! Now take care of it." (pp. 129–30)

One of the keys to success in the workplace is to learn how your boss or supervisor sees things and begin to apply those same perceptions, values, and standards to everything you do. This is even more important where "kingdom" business is concerned. Proper perspective can make the difference between success and failure every time. *Have you looked at your life through God's eyes lately? How do you measure up to God's biblical way of doing things?*

> Divine perspective changes everything and helps everything come into divine alignment. At times, the only way God can give you *His* view of your situation is to make you throw down everything that supports and encourages *your* view of life and ministry. (p. 130)

PRAYER

Lord, please forgive me for the times I've tried to contain You in some kind of formula that is the same every time. Your love, Your faithfulness, Your righteousness, and Your promises are eternally constant; but Your ways are infinitely variable. Grant me the wisdom and discernment to know when I should lay down all my burdens, goals, and commitments at Your feet; and when and how I should take them up again. In everything, I am reminded that You alone are God, and I am Your creation and adopted child.

Day 5

"I Didn't Know It Would Come to *This*"

> *How many times has He asked you to throw down your rod of comfort and security? What will you do if He asks you to lay down the security of a nine-to-five job with two checks per month and a liberal bonus package to pursue His impossible dream?*
>
> *If it hasn't happened already, I can promise you a holy encounter and a divine appointment are preordained in your destiny. God may not send you against an earthly prince or the head of a modern government, but He will almost certainly send you on a mission far beyond your ability.* (God's Eye View, p. 131)

SCRIPTURE READING

Exodus 3:11, where Moses eloquently expresses the way we all feel when God challenges us to do something we never expected (so what else is new?) by saying, "Who am I that I should go . . ."

WHILE IT IS TRUE that God is not limited to what we consider to be "logical," it amazes me how illogical we can be about God much of the time. Why would God ask us to do things we can do in our own strength and then try to get glory out of it? In most cases, He wouldn't and He doesn't (the one exception that comes to mind is His request that we say yes, and even that simple act probably requires divine grace).

I'm convinced the Lord purposely asks and leads us to do things beyond the limits of our own wisdom, ability, strength, and resources. *What has God put on your "plate" lately?*

When you feel overwhelmed and underequipped, you tend to grip the rod representing any lingering inner strength harder than usual. Throw it down, and cast your cares, fears, and doubts about His purposes at His feet as well.[2] (p. 132)

Are you clinging to something besides God at the moment? Are you determined to make "your plan" work at any cost? What if the cost is total disobedience to God or absolute failure? Release what you are clinging to and find new rest at His feet.

If you sense the need to magnify Him but mourn the loss of your magnifying glass, then return to the site of your last miracle or divine encounter. Throw down the rod of your strength and security in total dependence on Deity (and He will give you something far better). (p. 132)

PRAYER

Lord, at times I've felt as if I were dangling from a cliff while clinging to a small tree that is about to give way. I didn't know it would come to this, but now I realize that all along You were there with Your divine hand extended.

I cannot hold to both—I may continue clinging to my questionable handhold in my own strength as it crumbles before my eyes, or I may release my grip and surrender to the safety of Your hand. My decision is made, my grip released, my destiny secure. Thank You, Lord.

Don't Eat It—*Plant It!*

Moses had a change of attitude, and his rod had a change of ownership. Until that moment, Moses had leaned on the stick and called it his rod. Everything changed once he obeyed God and threw it down, watched it turn into a snake, and dared to pick it back up at God's command.

Before that moment, the rod was only strong enough for one man to lean on. Afterward, the rod of God represented a covenant relationship so strong that a whole nation depended on it. By God's will, it commanded enough power to open the Red Sea and bring Pharaoh to his knees. It pays to listen and obey when God asks you to release something or to pick up the unexpected. (God's Eye View, p. 133)

SCRIPTURE READING

2 Corinthians 9:10–11, where Paul says God supplies seed to planters and increases their store of seed so they can give generously on every occasion.

HARD TIMES AND difficult challenges seem to produce the damaging side effect of spiritual "tunnel vision." We begin to think, *It's God and me against the world.* God does love us, and He is intimately involved in every aspect of our lives (if we allow Him to be). Yet God's eye view also sees the situations of everyone near us.

When He blesses us, it is *never* for our benefit alone. He blesses us so that we may *be a blessing* in His name. *Has God blessed you recently? Did you make it a point to be a blessing in His name as well?*

God never works until it's too late and you're down to nothing. Remember that zero is the very best place to be—it's just hard to get there. The path to your personal zero point is also a journey to a supernatural seedtime and harvest.

In the natural realm, seedtime and harvest have a lot in common. In fact, their only outward difference is *quantity.* If it's not *enough*—it's seed! (Don't eat it—plant it!) (p. 134)

How many times have you received an obvious blessing from God, but were puzzled because whether or not it was supernaturally supplied, it still wasn't enough? Now you know what to do with it. It is seed corn—*plant it by faith* and trust God for an abundant harvest in due season. Look at it this way: either God is God or He is not. You and I must live and act according to our faith, and leave the rest to God.

PRAYER

Lord, You seem to keep taking me back to the law of sowing and reaping at every opportunity. I guess You are determined to help me learn and apply this law in every area of life. Let me begin with a simple seed planting right now: Lord, I surrender the seed of my life to You again, right now. Let me sink deeply into the rich soil of Your purposes and drink in the water of the Holy Spirit and the warm light from Your face. Cause me to produce blessings in the lives of everyone I meet from this day forward. Amen.

Look Up—Help Is on the Way

Worship is the greatest of all mood-altering drugs. It possesses the power to turn your darkest night into your brightest day. Worship will loose the winds of heaven to lift you on wings of praise into God's presence. Depression, discouragement, grief, and sorrow—they pale in power and influence when you begin to praise God, from whom all blessings flow. (God's Eye View, pp. 135–36)

SCRIPTURE READING

Luke 21:28, where Jesus ends His description of dire events in the end time with one of the most hope-filled declarations in all of the Bible: "Look up and lift up your heads, because your redemption draws near."

MOST OF US love good stories and movie plots that end well, especially those times when a key character faces great danger at the hands of some evildoer and the hero or heroine suddenly appears in the distance. We want to shout at the screen, "Don't give up, look up! Help is on the way, so don't quit now." In this case, art imitates life with God.

Worship! Right now! If God fails you, you will be the first person in history He's ever failed! (And I don't think you are important enough for Him to ruin His reputation over!) Keep on worshiping! Pick up the pieces and march on! (p. 136)

Do you feel as if something in your life has "slipped" or been lost somewhere between where you were and were you are right now?

Reclaim worship in your life and reenter the abundance of God's presence. Worship Him who holds your future and the destiny of the world in His hands. Allow the winds of the Spirit to lift you up to where you truly belong—in His presence.

PRAYER

Lord, I worship You because You are worthy. You are my Salvation, my Joy, my Hope, and my First Love. You are the Way, the Truth, and the Life—I stake all that I ever hope to be on You and Your unchanging Word. I lost my way, but I've reclaimed the worship reserved only for You. Lift me up, Father, to where I belong. Lift me up to heavenly places and help me see things with a God's eye view.

The Power of Proximity

Move Closer, Whisper Softer

God is almost "limited" by our ability to comprehend the incomprehensible. To illustrate just how close He wants us to come to Him, He chose to picture us in the two most intimate and beloved positions in human relationships—as His children and collectively as the bride of Christ.

As much as some of us wish God would have chosen less "embarrassing" and intimate examples, we can't change them and shouldn't even try. What does a son, a daughter, and a spouse do that no one else is entitled to do in private moments? They move close and whisper softer.

This is the privilege of proximity, and it comes only two ways—through blood relationship and covenant bond (as in the marriage covenant). We have both through the blood of Jesus Christ and the New Testament, or covenant, in His blood.

Do Whatever It Takes to Close the Distance

> *There are at least two ways to make something bigger to the eye.*
> *You can magnify it with a magnifying glass, microscope, or tele-*
> *scope; or you can move closer to it. Magnification makes an object*
> *appear larger to the eye, but there is only one way to get a sense of*
> *an object's true size in relation to you. You must move yourself closer*
> *or draw it close to you in some way. (God's Eye View, p. 137)*

SCRIPTURE READING
Hebrews 10:19–22, where the writer describes the "new and living way" of Jesus' blood that allows us to *draw near* to God.

EVEN AFTER WE have surrendered our lives to Jesus, we tend to make wrong decisions (or avoid the choices altogether when we shouldn't) and put "distance" between us and our God. It happens to the best of us despite the best of intentions.

This is the issue behind the warning in the Revelation to return to our First Love, and to be hot toward Him rather than lukewarm. *Do you sense a distance or a lukewarm apathy in your relationship with God? How did it happen?*

The cure for the lure of sin and apathy is simple but rare. Adopt a lifestyle of repentance. Make it your chief aim to please Him rather than displease Him. Consider His opinion and desires first, even before your own. *Would He be pleased to see you doing what you are thinking about doing?*

Stay hungry and always seek Him first. It starts by removing all the "empty filler" or easily forgotten busyness with which you fill your days. If you wonder what I'm talking about, try to remember what you did today . . . now yesterday . . . and the previous week. *Can you separate the empty filling from that with eternal value?*

Then do it. Do whatever it takes to move closer to the One who loves you and died for you. Magnify Him and fill your view with His glory. Move yourself closer to Him by fasting and denying everything that so easily distracts you. Worship Him and draw Him nearer to you. Do all three at the same time! Do what it takes to close the distance and dwell with Him.

PRAYER

Lord, I've made more than my share of mistakes and blunders, but at this moment I'm doing the right thing. I'm declaring my absolute hunger for You and my desire for Your presence. I'm determined to walk with You, even if it means changing my friendships and associations, my job, my habits and hobbies, my time allocation, and my lifestyle. I'm seeking You and Your kingdom first!

Day 2

When You Move Close, the Impossible Becomes Possible

> Praise is roughly similar to magnification. Worship, with its characteristic of intimacy and unconditional love, speaks of the power of proximity. When you link magnification of God with proximity or closeness to Him, He fills up your whole screen so that all you see is Him . . .
>
> Everything looks less intimidating when you are perched in Daddy's arms, viewing the world from His eye view. It also puts you in close proximity to Daddy's ear! And there's particular advantage to that position. (God's Eye View, pp. 138–39)

SCRIPTURE READING
Genesis 18:13–14, where God rebukes Sarah for laughing at His promise to do the impossible.

I'VE BEEN PREACHING since my teens, and I pastored a church for more than ten years before going on the road for thirty-plus years in traveling ministry. I'd always preached the Word of God the best I knew how and lived as holy as I could by the Holy Spirit. Yet, something new and wonderful happened to me one day in Houston, Texas.

I still ministered from the same Holy Bible, I was still married to the same wonderful wife, and I was still the father of three beautiful daughters. Yet I was different. In fact, I was probably a "worse" preacher by professional standards, because I kept interrupting my messages to cry and weep before God. The change had to do with *proximity*. *If you need a change, why don't you drop the formulas and programs and draw near to Him? He makes the impossible possible.*

> Have you ever noticed that some people seem to get their prayers answered more than others? It could almost make you suspect that God is a respecter of persons, but He said He isn't.[1]
>
> Is it because they pray right? Is it because they say it right? Is it because they have the right verbiage delivered at the right volume and strength? How many have tried all the different prayer and faith declaration methods only to say in the end, "I guess they're just better at it than I am"? . . .
>
> No, it is not that these people are "better" than you. *They may be closer.* If you can ever get *close,* anything is possible. I sense the Holy Spirit hovering over these words as I write. He's close to you now if you're worshiping as you read! (p. 139)

Although I was very well known within certain Christian circles, my ministry seemed to explode after my God encounter in south Texas. I wrote *The God Chasers* to describe what was happening and it rocketed to the best-seller list.

Was I a great writer? I think it was God's greatness showing through. He recognized my hunger (along with a lot of other hungry folks that day), and decided to demonstrate through me what happens when a professional preacher gets "too" close to Him. I was ruined for everything else but worshiping Him. *Are you ready to be ruined for everything else but worshiping Him? Draw near to Him.*

As for the ministry, we had to quickly expand our staff and scramble for more room. Then we had to do it again, and again! God wants us to draw close to Him, and He is blessing everyone who surrenders to Jesus and helps impart to others the hunger for His presence. *Remember, if you can get close to Him, anything is possible.*

PRAYER

Lord, I'm tired of spending the days of my life one at a time and having nothing to show for it. I want my life to matter in some way eternal. I'm hungry for You. I'm hungry to know You and show You to everyone I meet. Draw me close to You or please come close to Me so I will be changed to be more like You. Make the impossible possible through me, for Your glory.

Day 3

Don't Grow Content to Worship Him from Afar

I have a mental picture of you sitting at a table with Him enjoying a high tea together. He separated Himself from His usual celestial companions just to spend time with you and collect heavenly snapshots of the worship in your heart and in your eyes. As you sit at a table with Deity, you realize that many clamor to spend time with Him because of His fame and His power to bless and change human destiny.

Yet in that moment of intimacy at tea, He is your loving Father. You instinctively just stretch your hands out toward Him from time to time; at other times you suddenly realize all conversation has stopped, and you are simply gazing at Him in wonder over His love. (God's Eye View, p. 140)

SCRIPTURE READING
Matthew 19:14, where Jesus commands the disciples and professional preachers to make way or get out of the way so little children can come to Him.

IS YOUR WORSHIP LIFE with God giving your heavenly Father a series of treasured celestial snapshots of intimate moments of joy, or is He still waiting for you to look up from your work, your problems, your "ministry," and a thousand other earthly concerns?

Do you seek private moments with Him merely to present your shopping list, or do you mostly want to express your love for Him? Do you actively look for private moments in His presence or are you content to think of Him briefly from the safety of a pew or an upper balcony seat and then leave Him behind in some church building?

> The reality is that most people have never experienced such moments of intimacy with Divinity. Many who call themselves Christians have grown accustomed to living their lives feeling as if God was far away from them—an absentee father of sorts. (p. 141)

Many of us seem content to beg for small change in front of a posh seaside resort, when our name is on the register inside as a special guest of the Owner. We could be enjoying untold joys and refreshment in His presence if we took steps to seek Him, but instead many of us line up outside with our hands out, seeking and finding satisfaction in mere tokens of our inheritance in Him.

Are you ready for more? Will you pursue Him with passion, hunger, and determination? He just may allow Himself to be "caught" when you least expect it. Don't grow content to worship Him from afar when He bids you to "come closer."

PRAYER

Lord, I'm too desperate for Your presence to put up with anything less in my life. I'm willing to humble myself as a little child and run to You, even though others around me may criticize or ridicule my outrageous display of affection for You. All I know is that I love You and I will do anything to abide in Your presence.

Climb His Mountain—Don't Stop Short with Shortcuts

God always has done things from mountaintops. *Even in our day of modern convenience, self-reliance, and quick-service lifestyles, it seems His whole purpose is to get us and our problems to the top of His mountain so He can take care of it all. For our part, we tend to spend a lot of time looking for shortcuts, or else we simply stop short of His purposes.* (*God's Eye View,* p. 143)

SCRIPTURE READING
Genesis 22:1–18 and Exodus 20, describing the two times God called someone to come near or scale mountains where His presence was revealed.

GOD TESTED AND SEALED His covenant with Abraham and his seed on Mount Moriah, and revealed God's eye view on redemption there. Generations later, the children of Israel failed the mountain test near Mount Sinai.

When God called the people to come closer to His presence on Mount Sinai, they fell back in fear and sent Abraham instead (making him their shortcut to glory). It took thousands of years to overcome the damage caused by that shortcut to (or *away from*) God's presence.

The Lord's purpose was to establish such godly fear in their hearts that the people wouldn't sin—when they sent Moses forward when they should have come close themselves, they didn't get close enough to avoid sin or to fall in love with God.

We don't need to fall for the same mistake again. *God is calling you to come closer and scale His mountain . . . Are you willing to begin the climb, or are you still looking for a shortcut?*

Have you ever wondered whether there was any special significance to the name of the mountain Abraham climbed? According to James Strong, *Moriah* means "seen of Jah" (Jah is a contraction of the sacred Hebrew name of God).[2]

As far as I can tell, every word used in *Strong's Exhaustive Concordance of the Bible* to define the Hebrew root for "seen" supports an amazing conclusion: *Moriah* may also be translated or interpreted to mean "the mountain of God's eye view." (pp. 143–44)

Are you tired of viewing and experiencing life from the "tail end" of things? Isn't it time to climb the mountain of God? Worship God and allow Him to lift you up where you belong.

PRAYER

Lord, I discovered the truth about Your love for me and those like me. You planned from the beginning for us to be seated in heavenly places with You. I'm determined to scale the mountain of praise and worship to be with You—I'm no longer content to worship You from afar from the lowlands of mere human experience. You created me to be a worshiper, and I'm stepping into my divine destiny right now.

Leave the Lowlands of Low-Risk Worship—Aim for the Heights of God's Eye View

Jesus said, "Your father Abraham rejoiced to see My day."³ How can this be possible? How can a patriarch from the past see Jesus in the present and rejoice? From the mountain of God's-eye view you can see the past, the present, and the future. God did "provide Himself" as a lamb.

From the lofty heights of worship you can view your future—a future full of the provision of God. Keep climbing—keep worshiping!

That battle is always for Mount Moriah, the lofty place of God's-eye view. To this day, warring factions still contest that mountaintop. It's called in contemporary times "the Temple Mount," the seat of Judaism and Islam. There will always be a fight over the high place of worship. You need it, but Satan doesn't want you to get there. (God's Eye View, p. 145)

SCRIPTURE READING

John 9:1–34, where a blind man healed by Jesus is thrown out of the temple because he took the risky path; John 12:9–11, where Lazarus is added to the death warrant issued for Jesus; and Acts 4:13–20, where Peter and John are threatened because their risky actions and miracles made it clear "they had been with Jesus."

EXACTLY WHAT ARE the "risks of lofty worship"? You risk the displeasure, disapproval, and rejection of men and man-made religious systems, and you publicly align yourself with Jesus Christ, which makes His enemies *your* enemies. *It sounds risky, but ask yourself,* Is there any other path for a true Christian?

Consider the risky paths followed by the blind man healed in the temple, by Lazarus, who had been raised from the dead, and by Peter and John. *Their lives would never be the same—no longer were they able to walk into "first church" and pretend everything in the lowlands was fine.* If you choose the risky path to the heights of God's presence, you may find yourself unwelcome and unhappy in the low-risk environments of the status quo.

> *If we can ever worship at the height, we can return.* Far too often we get tired of exerting the energy and sacrifice it takes to get to that height.
>
> We decide to settle for secondary ascents and the ease of fast-food service. We opt for the lesser path and hang around the lowlands of low risk and blood-free worship. Then we wonder why we never see the solution to our problems. (p. 146)

Many Christians in nations where persecution and physical risk are automatic with any profession of faith in Christ pray diligently for believers in the United States and other relatively free nations. They believe it is harder to stand for Christ in a land of plenty than it is in a place of poverty and persecution. It is easier to take the low road of less risk and lower expectations than to climb the heights of risky worship and open passion to be in His presence.

There are no shortcuts, easy paths, or seven-step formulas to His presence. It takes passion, hunger, and one answer to His constant call to come higher: "Yes, Lord." *Which path will you take—the low road or the high road?*

PRAYER

Lord, the delicacies and ease of the lowlands no longer appease the burning hunger of my heart. I must risk all for the joy of Your presence. Obedience is my choice; risky all-out worship is my anthem. You chose me when You purchased my freedom and my eternal liberty on the cross; now I choose You.

Day 6

Only God Can See Both Sides of Your Problem Mountain

> *Abraham's problem and God's solution were coming up the same mountain, but the problem couldn't see the solution until it paid the price to reach the top. God was trying to direct Abraham to his destiny, but I'm sure Abraham couldn't help wondering, "Keep climbing? God, I don't understand. I want to know what happens once I get there." Abraham knew what God wanted him to do, even if he didn't understand the why of it all. Only God could see both sides of the mountain. (God's Eye View, p. 147)*

SCRIPTURE READING
Matthew 6:7–8, where Jesus says in simple terms that the Father sees both sides of our problems. He knows what we need—and has prepared provision for it—even before we ask for it.

GOD KNOWS OUR limitations—He generally allows us to see only what comes our way *today*. He knows we couldn't handle the pressure and faith required to foresee the future and then exercise faith for it in advance. We have enough trouble having faith for the moment, let alone for next month.

Your problem can't see God's solution until you pay the price for it. The great price was paid on Calvary; your price is measured in terms of daily obedience to His Word and Spirit, and the passionate pursuit of your First Love.

> Do you believe God has already spoken to the solution for your problems? It seems the solution often obeys His command better than the problem.

He has spoken to your "ram" as well, and He has predetermined the intersection point where you will meet His provision and solution. It is all laid out, so your job is to listen, obey, and do what it takes to get to that point. Worship Him, and draw near. If He can get you to keep going, you will find His ram waiting for your arrival. (p. 148)

Too much of the time, we waste precious time and energy questioning the character and Word of God. *He is gracious and full of mercy toward us, but shouldn't we be moving on from immaturity to maturity in our climb to His heights?*

"Father, how long should I climb? How far do I go?"

"Climb until you can't go anymore. Climb until you reach the end."

"Whose end?"

"Yours. Praise until you can't praise anymore. Worship until you have exhausted your abilities. That is where your problems meet His solution." . . .

You shouldn't be surprised—don't you see it? *He prearranged the rendezvous.* God has been waiting for you to reach the end of yourself so He can reveal *Himself.* Worship takes you from human weakness to divine strength, and finally into His glory on the mountain of God's-eye view. (p. 149)

PRAYER

Lord, I don't know the details right now, but I know that You love me and that You have supplied all I need to live a holy and victorious life.

My eyes are on You, and my heart burns for Your presence. I praise and worship You, and I willingly offer up my body, my soul, and my spirit as a living sacrifice to You.

Make me an instrument of Your presence in the earth, but let me abide under the shadow of Your wings for the rest of my days.

Day 7

Don't Offer Him Wimpy Worship—Worship Your Way to Moriah

> *It is time to worship, but not the wimpy worship that stops simply when the clock hits twelve noon. It is time to worship your way to Moriah, the land of God's-eye view. Worship and praise your way up the mountain of the Lord, and don't settle for anything less than a mountaintop encounter with the joy of your heart's desire. (God's Eye View, p. 155)*

SCRIPTURE READING
Psalm 138, the God Chaser's psalm of total dedication, trust, and passionate worship.

I'VE DISCOVERED THAT the more I praise and worship God, the bolder I become. Many people wrongly assume that "worship people" stay mostly indoors, holding so-called revival services, and that they don't mingle with unsaved folks. The truth is that people exposed to God's glory are impossible to shut down, shut up, or shove aside. They won't be denied; they can't help themselves; they are burning to tell others about God's glory and grace.

Have you noticed that God uses "worship people" to ignite revival with their passion? (I've never seen or read of a revival ignited by stale theology or empty religious ritual.) *Where will He find you—ready and burning, or already turning stale?*

If your Christian life lacks power, you won't find it in a formula or seven *easy* steps to Christian success. You will find it in determined praise, uninhibited repentance and surrender, and the willingness to worship your way all the way onto God's altar and into close *proximity* to His heart.

I think I know what you're thinking, but I read somewhere, "I beseech you therefore, brethren, by the mercies of God, *that you present your bodies a living sacrifice, holy, acceptable to God,* which is your reasonable service."[4] (p. 155)

The modern church, especially in many affluent Western industrialized nations, appears to have fallen far from the mark established by the first-century churches in Jerusalem and Antioch. The closest thing we have to power is what comes through the power line. We've spent decades and centuries searching for shortcuts and formulas. Now it's God's turn.

He is calling all of us upward. It is privilege in Christ to worship and praise our way up the mountain of the Lord, but we must not settle for anything less than a world-changing encounter with the Joy of our heart's desire.

PRAYER

Here I am Lord; I've come again with thanksgiving on my lips, with praise in my heart, just worshiping You with all that I am.

It is true that I can't see very well from my earthly viewpoint, but now I've taken wing in the midst of praise and worship for You. Lift me up where I belong, at Your side with a hymn of praise and a blood-bought song.

My goal is nothing less than the spiritual Mount Moriah, where You will supply me with a God's-eye view of the kingdom and all that concerns me. This is the heritage of all who answer the call to draw near and bring You worship.

Claim Your Backstage Pass

Worship Your Way to God's Eye View

If you have ever attended a play, a musical, or a concert, you understand the value of a backstage pass. It is a passport, a key of entry into the behind-the-scenes world screened from the general audience. It gives you direct access to the principal players, the stage director, and even the script at times.

Access to backstage passes is carefully screened and protected, and most of the time only those in direct relationship to the players, the producers, or the production process itself gain such privileged access.

The blood of Jesus Christ and the act of worship are a celestial backstage pass onto the stage of eternity. It is there that you gain access to the counsels of God and see the players for who they really are.

You have access to the script and to the unfolding finale in the last act. This privileged access changes your view of world events forever. You know the ending. Now the frightening antics of the antagonist have been reduced to mere playacting by a lizard in a badly fitting suit. This only happens for those who worship their way to a God's eye view.

Wailers See the Problem; Worshipers See the Solution

From John's limited earthly perspective, it seemed that destiny hung in the balance because no one was worthy to open the seals of the scroll. Even though John was seeing a heavenly vision set in the very throne room of God, the outcome was so uncertain that the apostle of the church cried almost uncontrollably!

What happened to this veteran of countless encounters with religious leaders, the emperor of Rome, and Satan himself? What crisis could reduce this great spiritual leader and intercessor to tears? . . .

John became nervous and was overcome by anxiety because he didn't know how things would end! Remember that John honestly recorded what he saw with such detail that it almost seems as if he jotted down notes as he saw them. (God's Eye View, pp. 159–60)

SCRIPTURE READING
Hebrews 12:2, where we are told from yet another perspective to "fix our eyes on Jesus, the author and perfecter of our faith" (NIV).

IT IS LEGITIMATE for those in intercession to weep and "wail" over the predicaments and problems of those for whom they pray; *however*, many of us major in wailing about a problem when we should focus more on worshiping the One who is our Divine Solution.

The situation of the apostle John as he viewed the scene around God's throne is a lesson for us in the virtue and necessity of God's eye view over man's viewpoint of things.

One of the heavenly beings stepped away from the celestial worship circle just long enough to lean over the tearful apostle and give him a tip about God's end-time script:

> So I wept much, because no one was found worthy to open and read the scroll, or to look at it. But *one of the elders* said to me, *"Do not weep. Behold, the Lion of the tribe of Judah,* the Root of David, has prevailed to open the scroll and to loose its seven seals."[1] (p. 162)

How many times have you sensed the Holy Spirit "interrupting" your private and personal pity party to say in essence, "Look up—Jesus is right in front of you with an eternity of comfort and a universe full of abundant supply"? What did you do next?

John's problem and the angelic correction provide us with this simple truth about where we place our focus in life and in our walk with God:

> The one who was wailing had his eyes on the problem, and the one who was worshiping had his eyes on the Solution. (p. 163)

Which one are you?

PRAYER

Lord, I've done more than my share of wailing over problems, failures, and difficulties. Now I'm ready for a change of view, for a new perspective of old problems and the obstacles before me right now. My eyes are on You. Lift me up where I belong and let me see things from Your viewpoint.

Day 2

Sit with God or Sit in the Cheap Seats with Satan

> *Your great High Priest says to you and to me, "I know how it looks from the perspective of the audience! I know how you feel, but I have a better place and a better seat reserved for you." (God's Eye View,* p. 164)

SCRIPTURE READING
Luke 23:42–43, where one of the thieves crucified beside Jesus asks for and receives a personal invitation to a much better seat in eternity than the one he has on earth.

DO THINGS LOOK bad for you right now? Do you feel trapped and doomed to live in failure or embarrassment for the rest of your days?

The thief couldn't have had a worse view of life and death as he gasped for breath on a Roman cross. Death for him was guaranteed just before sundown at the latest, and he had two choices—curse God and die (the option chosen by the other thief), or believe God and live. He asked Jesus to remember him, but the Lord did for him what He did for us—He gave him a "backstage pass" to the mystery play of life.

Things aren't so rosy for the arch rebel and those who follow him down the wide and easy path of rebellion.

> Satan has an eternity-long box seat in the back row of the theater of God. He can't figure out what's going on, he's powerless to change or modify God's script, and if he could read God's script (he does know how to quote a few lines here and there), he still wouldn't understand it. He doesn't have the key

151

to understanding the Word—the Holy Spirit. He can't even get good popcorn—all he ever gets is the burned stuff at the bottom with a hint of sulfur flavoring. (p. 165)

Why do I spend so much time and space describing Satan's limited options? It is because his options are *our options* if we fail to follow the Son of God in life and in death.

Do you sometimes feel as if Satan's misery has become *your* misery? *Do you feel powerless to change or modify the "script" of your life? Do you want to shout and shake your fist at God over your troubled childhood, the color of your skin, the poverty in your family, or your limited options in life?*

I have two things to say to you. First, Jesus understands your anger, your frustration, and your pain. That is why He came to take your place on the tree of blame. Second, you are *not* powerless to change your destiny as long as you retain the power of choice.

The thief on the tree was out of options—he was beyond the forced solitude of death row, he was "in the chair" and minutes from death. Yet he exercised the power of choice and chose Jesus Christ. That brief thirty-second exchange with Jesus changed his eternity from doom and damnation to eternal joy! *Are you still breathing? Then you still have the power of choice—choose now* (and trust the rest to Him).

PRAYER

Lord, I choose You. I know I've failed, I've sinned, I've made one wrong choice after another for as long as I can remember. I feel as if I'm hanging on a cross right now, but then I saw You. I choose You.

Will You lift me off this cross and take me with You? With the help of the Holy Spirit, I will follow wherever You lead from this moment on— even if I've already "tried it" and failed once before.

Ignorance Is *Not* Bliss

This is what worship does for you: it provides you with privileged access to Deity's secrets, the divine mysteries and hidden wisdom of God that Satan cannot even begin to understand. Even the angels in heaven—let alone the fallen angelic prince called Satan—cannot understand the mystery of God . . .

Satan does not want you to understand heavenly perspective either. If he can't ascend the hill of the Lord ever again, then he is determined to keep anyone else from doing it. He doesn't want you to understand that the higher you fly in worship, the smaller he becomes and the larger your Father appears in your view. (God's Eye View, pp. 165–66)

SCRIPTURE READING

2 Corinthians 2:11, where the apostle Paul warns us to forgive so Satan won't take advantage of us, and adds, "for we are not ignorant of his devices."

IT IS DEITY'S LOVE for fallen humanity that mystifies the angels above and below. It also seems to mystify us much of the time. Perhaps that is why we sometimes seem so reluctant to extend the same privileges of forgiveness and a new start to other people.

Nevertheless, we are to forgive one another and even the unsaved people who may be persecuting us, just as He forgave us. Anything less provides Satan with a legitimate weapon to use against us.

Judging by your willingness to forgive others, have you acted with knowledge of God's grace or in "ignorance of Satan's devices"?

Your backstage seat in heavenly places provides the difference between sitting in the dark with the audience and being on the stage with the players and the heavenly script at your fingertips for reference into the future.

People in the earthly audience may get nervous or distraught because they don't know the script. If you are on stage and you know the players, if you have the counsel of Him who knows the end from the beginning, then you won't be nervous about any of it! The celestial villain could jump out and scare the audience out of their seats, but his antics won't bother you because you know his end. (p. 167)

Are you tired of living in fear and suspense over the next "bad thing" that will happen to you? Forgive others unconditionally and begin to worship the One who forgave you. Allow the wings of worship to lift you above the confusing swirl of life and get God's eye view of your life and your place in His purposes.

Once you see things from God's perspective, the devil's antics won't bother you anymore—*you've read the end of the Book, and you're sitting next to the Author.*

PRAYER

Dear Lord, I am spreading my wings of worship to catch the updraft of the Holy Spirit. I know that the higher I fly in worship, the smaller the enemy becomes and the larger You are in my eyes and heart. I will live and worship according to Your eternal counsel, Lord, for You know the end from the beginning. Fear must flee in the face of my Redeemer! I am in hot pursuit of Your face, Lord.

Day 4

The Nearsighted Devil Meets the Farsighted God

> *Difference in perspective has played a crucial role in God's plans and purposes since the very beginning of time. The human race is not alone in its perspective-challenged state.* Satan suffers from perpetual spiritual myopia; *he is so nearsighted that he cannot see one millimeter beyond the veil of holiness and the mystery of the gospel.* (God's Eye View, p. 167, emphasis added)

SCRIPTURE READING
1 Corinthians 2:6–12, where Paul describes in seven brief sentences the mystery of God hidden from the spiritual vision–challenged devil and the unsaved.

HAVE YOU EVER WONDERED why the Old Testament prophets and the apostle Paul called God's redemption plan a "mystery"? Many of us wonder what all the mystery is about, and we almost take it for granted. One reason it is called a mystery is that it is *still* a mystery to Satan and the hellish hosts, as well as to the angels in heaven.

The immeasurable love of the Creator, who is everything for incredibly self-centered created beings who seem to be almost nothing, is baffling to angels, to say the least. On the face of it, we are glorified bags of enriched water with a few minerals thrown in. We are here today and gone tomorrow on the eternal clock.

Why does God care? He cares because He created us in His own image for a divine purpose. *Why does God care about you?* He cares specifically about you because He created *you* for a specific divine purpose too.

If anything should help us put Satan in the proper perspective as a defeated and humiliated fallen angel, it is the mystery of the gospel.

> Divinity counted on the limited access of Satan and his fallen cohorts. That is one of the reasons Jesus walked through His earthly ministry as a man. As the psalmist said, He "delivered His strength into captivity, and His glory into the enemy's hand."[2] (p. 168)

As we noted earlier, Satan has *limited access* to God's ear and *no* access to God's power and glory. That is reserved for *you* and *me*. Satan never dreamed in his worst nightmare (and he's had some *bad* ones) that God would actually sacrifice His own Son to make you and me His children! That is the nightmare that keeps on tormenting . . .

Since Jesus delivered His strength into captivity to save you, *are you willing to deliver your strength into His hands now?* If He willingly released His own glory just to set you free from sin, *are you willing to release your glory, your pride, and your ambition into His hands for divine purposes?*

PRAYER

Lord, I surrender all to You. There are no conditions, no "buts," no legal provisos, exceptions, or limitations. You gave everything for me, so the least I can do is give everything I am back to You.

All I want is You. I want to see Your face, to rest in Your presence, and to dwell in Your glory. Thank You for making me Your child through the blood of Jesus.

Day 5

The Elder Saw Costumed Strength in Captivity

> *The elder knew the secret: the appearance of the Lamb was all part of God's orchestrated plan. He knew that wasn't really a lamb opening the seals. That was the Lion of Judah who had put on the garment and costume of a lamb. It was strength in costumed captivity! (God's Eye View, p. 169)*

SCRIPTURE READING
Revelation 5:5–6, where a celestial elder reveals that the Lamb is a Lion in divine disguise.

THE PROPHETS OF OLD must have scratched their heads when God spoke such puzzling things and blended seemingly opposing pictures together. These apparently conflicting portraits of the plan of God painted by the ancient prophets are so opposite one another that the students of their prophecies must have devoted years of study trying to decipher the divine code of redemption. What was the key to this holy conundrum? We are still trying to comprehend its wonder today.

How do the "Lamblike" virtues of Jesus our Savior join together in your life with the "Lionlike" virtues of Jesus, the King of kings? The answer is not found in an idea, philosophy, concept, or ethical construct—it is found in the living person of Jesus Christ, the Son of God.

> As a member of an earthbound audience, you may weep and wonder, "Look at the weakness of the Lamb! I don't understand how God can help me with One so weak." The secret of the

157

mystery is that God's strength is made perfect in our human weakness.[3] (p. 169)

Every day, the God in you, Emmanuel, reveals His "costumed strength in captivity" in the body of another lamb—a lamb that goes by *your name*. His strength really is made perfect in your weakness—if you yield to Him. *"How can my weaknesses reveal God to the people around me?"*

People aren't stupid. They know how people normally react to rejection, hatred, failure, sickness, or financial reversals. They know how they would react to problems in a marriage or on the job.

What they *don't know* is why you react *differently* to those things when it is clear it still hurts! *The answer is the Lion living inside your lamb suit.*

PRAYER

Lord, I give up. The truth is that I am not as strong as I pretend to be. I'm not as holy or brave or loving as I say I am either. In fact, the only good things in me are the things You put in me directly or through other godly people You've placed in my life.

I know this much—You are living in my heart and life. Show Your strength through my weakness, Lord. This lamb is leaning on You with all of its heart, soul, and strength. Show them the Lion of Judah hidden inside the captivity of my weak lamb costume.

Day 6

He Killed Divinity's Disguise and Unleashed the Christ

> *No, that wasn't just another prophet. That was the Lamb slain according to the sacred script before the foundations of the world. All Satan did the day he killed the Lamb was to unveil the Lion! Ask John.*
>
> *What looks like a lamb from our perspective is really a lion from God's-eye view. When Satan killed the flesh of Jesus the Lamb, he unleashed the power of Christ, the Lion of Judah. All the devil managed to do was to kill Divinity's disguise. (p. 174)*

SCRIPTURE READING
Genesis 3:14–15, where God forecasts frequent and fatal headaches for a cosmic heel-bruiser in a picture of the great conflict on Mount Calvary.

WHAT HAPPENS WHEN *the enemy of your soul arouses persecution against you or tempts you to the point of failure?* He would like for you and everyone around you to think "he won." That is exactly what he tried to say about the Crucifixion on Calvary. The devil just can't get it into his head that he is reenacting the same mistake he made at Calvary two thousand years ago.

Every time your adversary comes against you or tries to kill something in you, the moment you turn it over to the Lord, the Christ in you, the Lion of Judah, is revealed. Satan killed the Son of God in a single human body, but reaped a harvest of the Son of God dwelling in untold millions of human bodies through the Holy Spirit—*including yours.*

Are you a part of the devil's recurring nightmare or are you part of his "luke-warm, half-dead Christian" insider team? If you lean on the Lamb of God in your weakness, then every time the devil strikes you, he is striking the heel of Jesus, and a crushing boot comes down on his head with crushing force.

When Satan strikes you as a lamb of God's flock, your surrendered life in Christ makes you part of the devil's inescapable recurring nightmare. (You would think he would learn after two millennia.) *The bottom line is that Satan gets a crushing headache from God and unleashes the power of Christ every time he tries to bruise you. That's what happens when someone tries to touch one of God's kids.*

PRAYER

Lord, I've laid down every claim I have about being strong, wise, independent, or self-sufficient. My strength is found in Your strength. Jesus Christ is made Wisdom to me. I am not independent; I am a branch linked up eternally to the Vine. My strength and my boast are in my weakness, and my total dependence is upon Jesus the Lamb of God, the Lion of Judah, the risen King of kings.

Day 7

Lions, Babes, and a Lizard "in Drag"

Spread your wings of worship so you can fly high enough to take your seat beside Him and look out of the portals of heaven. Get a God's-eye view and divine perspective of your situation.

Is it really possible? Can I do that, or is this just another nice teaching meant for the sweet by-and-by?

Don't take my word for it. Read it for yourself in God's Word. The apostle Paul declared under the inspiration of the Holy Spirit:

> *God, who is rich in mercy, because of His great love with which He loved us, even when we were dead in trespasses, made us alive together with Christ (by grace you have been saved), and raised us up together, and made us sit together in the heavenly places in Christ Jesus.*[4]

(God's Eye View, p. 179)

SCRIPTURE READING

Galatians 4:6–7, where Paul describes how God sent the Spirit of His Son into our hearts so we could cry, "Daddy, Father," and be heirs of the kingdom with Jesus.

DISAPPOINTMENT EXERTS a powerful force on the human heart. It makes your hopes fade and buries your dreams in pain. In contrast, eternal truth is a fortress rooted in God's faithfulness that will not fail or be denied. It stands against the disappointments of life on earth with unshakable strength.

Emotions are a natural part of being human, but emotions were never meant to rule or anchor your life on earth. That role is reserved for God's Word because it never changes or fails.

When pain, rejection, or disappointment threatens to overwhelm you, are you tempted to go by how you *feel* about yourself or the problem? Don't fall for it. Go by what *God says* about you or your situation. Things are not always as they seem . . .

> God doesn't want you *down* looking *up*. He wants you *up* looking *down*. When you worship Him and take your seat in His presence, this is what you will discover:

> The Lamb is a Lion,
> the Babe is the Ancient of Days, and
> the Dragon is really a lizard.

(p. 179)

Worship opens the door for the light of heaven to flood your life and circumstances. His light has a way of revealing the truth behind every circumstance. You will discover, with John, that the Lamb is actually a Lion, and the Babe of the manger is really the Ancient of Days.

You also realize that the thing masquerading as a dragon that threatens your life and steals your peace is nothing more than a lizard "in drag," something pretending to be something else in a ridiculous charade.

Are you tired of running from an overblown lizard when the Lion lives in you? Will you throw down the lie that Jesus Christ is less than what He truly is? That the truth is, the risen Son of God is well able to finish the good work He began in you?

Yes, it is really possible to spread your wings of worship and soar in His presence. Yes, it is your destiny. Come on up and worship Him.

PRAYER

Father, I worship You and magnify Your name. Through the Spirit of Jesus living in my heart, I cry out, "Abba, Daddy!" in the privileged access You only extend to Your blood-bought children. Lift me up where I belong, seated with my Lord in heavenly places. I can see clearly now in the light of Your presence—the Lamb is a Lion, the Babe is the Ancient of Days, and the dragon is really a lizard. Blessed be the name of the Lord.

Costumed Characters

The Lamb Is a Lion,
the Babe Is the Ancient of Days,
the Dragon Is a Lizard

The human mind and memory tend to work with "burned in" images or location points that stand out. A frightening scene, dream, or sound may haunt human dreams for a lifetime. The memory of a first kiss or the smell of a mother's perfume usually follows us all our days.

God has given us three pictures of "costumed characters" that define the greatest mystery and cosmic conflict of all time. He pictures Jesus Christ as a humble Lamb sent to the slaughter, who emerges from the grave with the roar of the Lion of Judah. Jesus is also remembered as the tender Babe in a manger, who is also the Ancient of Days who has always existed. Finally he strips away the daunting description of the deadly dragon, who is really a scurrying lizard whose days are numbered.

These pictures and images close the book and seal the "ending" on God's mysterious plan to deliver His creation from evil. They should forever change our perspective of life and eternity—now we see things from *God's Eye View.*

"Wook, Daddy, Widdle Debbil All Dwessed Up"

Just as we went through the front gate, a big seven-foot blue TV
character bounced over to shake my daughter's hand. She climbed
me like I was a tree. (God's Eye View, p. 183)

SCRIPTURE READING

2 Timothy 1:7, where Paul speaks to fearful tree-climbers of all
ages about how to overcome fear with a God's-eye view through
His spirit of power, love, and a sound mind.

MOST OF US won't admit it publicly, but we've climbed our own share of
trees in moments of terror, fear, and panic. A seven-foot blue TV character may not faze us, but a three-ounce malignant tumor or a pink slip will
usually do the trick.

The tree-climbing usually starts with much less dramatic surprises. It
may be triggered by personal rejection by a friend or coworker, or by an
arithmetic error on an IRS form that produces one of those heart-stopping
notices delivered by an innocent postal employee. It may be a late-hour
attack by a fearful thought; it may be a startling thought about death and
the brevity of human life. In any case, fear is its foundation.

> We shouldn't be flinching like other people do when the
> antagonist of our race makes an attack on us. We've read the
> back of the book; we've seen the final act, and we know who
> wins. (p. 182)

The "C word" (cancer) strikes fear into the hearts of hundreds of thousands of North Americans every year, and the fear it produces seems to be virtually as fatal as any of the forms of that dreaded disease. Fear paralyzes us, but love releases and empowers us, and *perspective* can make all the difference.

> She was so scared that her little body just shook—until that young man leaned into that grille and said softly, "Hi, baby." The instant she could see his eyes, she could see that he was just a young boy.
>
> I said, "See, baby, that's just a little boy all dressed up in costume."
>
> The rest of the day, whenever my little girl saw somebody in costume, she'd grab my hand and she'd look at me, then she'd say, "Wook, Daddy. Widdle boys all dwessed up." (p. 184)

The next time Satan attacks you, your family, or your local church body, *what will you do? Will you look for the nearest natural tree to climb or climb the Tree of Golgotha for a God's-eye view?*

PRAYER

Lord, I rarely want to reveal it to people, but You already know the truth—things get to me sometimes. When it happens, I'd just rather give up, go home, and stay there. The problem is that You didn't call us to stay shut up behind closed doors all the time. You called us to live in a higher place, enjoying a God's-eye view of our destiny and purpose in Your grand passion. Lift me up where I belong so I can do what You called me to do all along—to worship You and obey Your commands.

Privileged Living in the High-Rise of God

> *There is a place in God, a secure path in the Living Way, where*
> *you cannot be touched no matter how much Satan tries to reach and*
> *claw at you. It is a level of intimacy with Divinity that would be*
> *fatal to anyone but God's children and the angels who serve Him.*
> *The only problem is that His level isn't our level.*
>
> *Although Jesus paid the total price for our salvation with His life*
> *and His blood, we must pay the price for intimacy with Divinity by*
> *laying down our lives daily. (God's Eye View, p. 188)*

SCRIPTURE READING
Isaiah 35:8–10, where the prophet describes a highway of holiness, speaking of Jesus, where the righteous walk but the predator
is denied access.

CITY DWELLERS have completely different ideas about "the good life"
from people who live in less crowded conditions in more rustic settings.

Many people in New York, Chicago, downtown Los Angeles, or
Houston value a penthouse view in a high-rise condominium far more
than they appreciate a broad country estate. They especially like the views
above the din and danger of the city streets, and they value the *exclusivity*
and *security* of their elevated dwelling places. Most of them would be willing to make great sacrifices to live in such places.

God has prepared a place of untouchable security in Christ for those
who give up everything to follow Him. *Is there anything in your life you are*
unwilling to give up for the privilege of serving in Christ's high-rise community?

Jesus didn't ask us to climb on *His* cross to pay for our own salvation because we could not and cannot pay that price. But once we make the choice to follow Him, He commands us to take up *our own* cross and follow Him.

Are you content to warm a pew the rest of your life, or will you pay the price of true discipleship to walk the High Way and acquire a God's-eye view?

> The church has entered a season when hunger, holiness, and servanthood are supplanting the lesser values of satisfaction, conformity to religious rituals, and kingdom building. (p. 191)

When I say "the church" has entered this season of "hunger, holiness, and servanthood," you must understand that the corporate church body obeys and serves God *one member at a time.*

Revival comes when enough individual believers say, "Yes, Lord," to start a fire with the sparks they strike between them. *Are you saying "Yes," or are you saying "Not now"?*

PRAYER

Lord, I'm not content to live the low life by warming a pew all of my days. You gave me life for a reason; I was born to fulfill a divine destiny as part of Your purposes in the earth. I'm willing to pay the price—help me take my cross today. Grant me the grace to deny myself and follow You unconditionally. You are my Great Reward; Your presence is my chief joy. By following hard after You, I pursue my greatest desire.

"I Quit! Get Me Off This Operating Table!"

If you fail to yield to God's rebuilding and repair process, you will never become the receptacle for that whole process; you've short-circuited everything that God can do. And you can stop being embarrassed about sowing seed. God is "repairing the nets," and He's getting ready to send us out for a final midnight run. That's when you get those net-breaking catches we read about in the Scriptures. (God's Eye View, p. 192)

SCRIPTURE READING
Amos 9:11, where the prophet describes God's rebuilding and restoration work in His favorite restaurant, the tabernacle of David.

IF YOU HAVE a few minutes, ask someone you know who experienced the labor of natural childbirth about her memories of that scene. Doctors, nurses, and midwives refer to one particular stage of childbirth as "transition" because it marks the clear-cut passage from one phase of labor into the final stage of delivery. There is no turning back once you enter transition.

I'm told that one of the telltale signs of transition is the mother's compelling urge to tell everyone in attendance, "I quit! I want out. Let's stop this and go home." By then it is too late—mother and child are committed until the end. *Do you feel a compelling desire to tell God, "I quit. Get me off this operating table"?*

God isn't fickle or double-minded as people are. Once He begins a good work in us, He completes it (no matter how loud or how long we scream).

The Great Physician knows exactly what we need at any given time, regardless of what we *think* we need. However, you still have the ability to stop or hinder the process, and most of us *like* to make our own decisions about what is best for us.

If you try to stop God's process in the midst of transition, you may risk aborting God's purpose for the process. Much of our pain in life is self-induced because we constantly search for shortcuts to the process of God.

Sometimes He must break us down before He can build us up. He may cut away something deadly before He repairs us and reforms us into what we were born to be. *Are you tempted to cut short God's repair and remodeling plans in your life? Are you prepared to abort the supernatural harvest He sends to those who wait upon Him and His purposes?*

Don't quit. You've set your hand to the plow, so don't look back now. The harvest is just around the corner.

PRAYER

Father, I repent for my attempts to escape Your correction or shorten my time under Your guiding and reforming hand. Forgive me for trying to quit when You want me to push. My life is Yours; direct my steps so I will be a worker, a harvester, and a servant in whom You are well pleased.

Day 4

Worship, Worship, Worship—God Loves It (Do You?)

Some would like to lump together all of my ideas about God Chasers, God Catchers, and the passionate pursuit of His presence and file them under one tidy classification in their exhaustive but handy religious handbooks. I suspect the file heading would read: "Tenney, Tommy—upstart Louisiana preacher who talks endlessly about worship, worship, worship. Known to preach in almost any-body's church." (God's Eye View, p. 193)

SCRIPTURE READING
Revelation 15:4, where John describes the attendees at an end-time worship service.

OUR RELIGION-BOUND ideas about worship are so rigid and lifeless in some cases that it takes nothing less than a supernatural explosion to break us free. Our love of sameness and unchanging ritual forces the Builder of the church to extreme measures of demolition to introduce anything that hints of change.

The truth is that worship changes and adapts as people change and adapt. Charles Wesley was regarded as an outrageous rebel in his day for daring to adorn "Top 40" bar-song melodies with sacred words and biblical theology.

The established church bucked the trend, but today Wesley's hymns often *are* the established form, while anything new or different from them is outrageous and unacceptable. *How do you feel when someone proposes different music, or introduces unusual forms of worship in "your" service?*

> They would be right about my focus, but dead wrong about my *definition* of worship . . . In this season worship begins the moment you say *yes* to every task, service, project, or activity instigated by God's Word and the Holy Spirit. (p. 193)

We must broaden our perspective of worship to match God's eye view. Who would call it worship if someone walked up to an altar, fell to his knees, took off his hat, and suddenly threw it on the floor? Would it be worship if a policeman threw his badge and gun toward the altar? *What were the "twenty-four elders" doing in Revelation 4:10–11?*

Worship truly begins with the word *yes* and moves forward from there. *Are you saying "yes," "maybe," or "not me" right now?*

One of our biggest mistakes is the tendency to quantify, qualify, and categorize the people of God and the things of His kingdom. Whenever we feel we "understand" something, we also feel we have earned the right to dismiss things. "I've been to that seminar, bought that T-shirt, and the tape set is in the bottom shelf of my library. Don't need to go there again." We couldn't be more wrong when it comes to worship. That *is exactly* where we are going in eternity.

PRAYER

Lord, You created me to be a worshiper first, and everything else comes after that. May I never forget or minimize that fact. Forgive me for the times I put my job, my ministry, my family, my problems, or my friends ahead of my first ministry and duty in this life—to worship You.

Day 5

Has God Hidden You in the Bulrushes?

This is a key moment in the divine timetable. Once again Satan is holding his head, and he can't figure it out. Somewhere the anointing is rising, and he fears he won't be able to stamp out this holy fire either. God has an entire generation of deliverers hidden in the bulrushes around His river of life. (God's Eye View, p. 194)

SCRIPTURE READING

Esther 4:14, where a man speaks to the unlikely deliverer of a nation and says, "Who knows whether you have come to the kingdom for such a time as this?"

EVERY TIME THE DEVIL thinks it is safe to scheme and plot against the purposes of God, he discovers in painful ways that God has a deliverer waiting to crush his plans and bruise his rebellious head.

First, he ran into a series of smaller deliverers who ruined his day. Then the Great Deliverer came to issue eviction orders and seize the keys of the hellish house. Now he feels the heat of God's rising once again. He's running into an entire generation of deliverers who walk, talk, command, and wreak havoc on darkness just like Jesus. What's a devil to do?

The real question is, What are you going to do? Will you pursue God's presence and allow yourself to become a carrier of His holy fire, or will you step aside to let your flame go out in the name of ease and comfort?

The enemy may be aware that his end is near, but he is not about to cave in or give up. He is doing everything he can to divert, dampen, discourage, divide, and desensitize God's people. He has things the way he likes them, so he tries desperately to stop people who want to impose God's kingdom on areas of darkness. *Is the enemy of your soul actively opposing you, or are you so nonthreatening and powerless in his view that he doesn't have to oppose you?*

You weren't given life merely to live and die, accomplishing nothing. *Who knows whether you have come to the kingdom for such a time as this?*

PRAYER

Lord, I acknowledge that You knew me by name even when I was still in my mother's womb. I surrender to Your plans and will for my tomorrows—be glorified in me. Call me out of the bulrushes and set my soul on fire in Your presence. Anoint me with power from on high to bring deliverance to the captives in Jesus' name.

Day 6

Restored and Seeing Everything Clearly

We need God's-eye view in every area of life. We've limped along with hampered vision long enough.

If you had a choice between impaired sight or 20/20 vision for the rest of your life, which would you choose? That is the choice God sets before us now. (God's Eye View, pp. 194–95)

SCRIPTURE READING

Mark 8:22–25, where Jesus heals a blind man, but only after He prayed for him a second time because he said, "I see men like trees, walking." When Jesus prayed the second time, the man "was restored and saw everyone clearly."

TAKE A STROLL through church history from the first century to the present and try to describe what you see. The ups and downs, the sidetracks, dead stops, backtracking, and sudden jumps are enough to make anyone wonder if "those people" were sane and whole or not.

The significant jumps forward in the Divine purpose usually came through the lives of people with clear spiritual vision and insight. Impaired vision seems to account for the wildly exaggerated swings on the pendulum of faith. *How is your spiritual eyesight? Are you limited to see-ing "me, myself, us four, and no more," or are you able to see God's hand mov-ing through the greater church that spans cultures, languages, and generations?*

The church family has endured some nearly fatal swings toward the flesh and heresy. It happened during the rule of Roman emperor Constantine and it also happened during the Dark Ages (to name only two of many instances).

The American church faced a similar situation early in our history when a profanity movement swept through universities formerly founded to train ministers of the gospel. It took a mighty move of God through the Great Awakening to turn the nation around and *restore our spiritual vision* once again.

What about you? Are you tired of going through life with hampered spiritual vision? If you are ready to enjoy the benefits of "20/20 spiritual vision," then worship God. Allow Him to lift you up where you belong so you can see things with God's eye view.

PRAYER

Lord, heal my spiritual eyes and lift me higher so that I can see clearly. Make my steps sure and my vision clear. I fix my eyes on You and worship You. Thank You for allowing me to see things from a heavenly perspective through Your Word and by Your Spirit. Thank You for restoring me so I can see everything clearly.

Day 7

God's Eye View Brings Joy in the Face of Hopelessness

> *It has been said that some of the Christians who died as martyrs in Rome's Colosseum left this life singing hymns of joy to God. They had a God's-eye view of a situation that seemed hopeless at the ground level of life without God. (God's Eye View, p. 195)*

SCRIPTURE READING

Matthew 28:8–9, where the sorrow of a tomb and the joy of divine encounter are met together in a supernatural juncture of hopelessness and He who is our Hope.

CHRISTIANS HAVE THE ABILITY to completely lose sight of truth in the defense of their *interpretations* of truth. Believers have come to blows over their respective views of end-time passages in the Scriptures while totally missing the point that it is all about the Prince of Peace and the kingdom of joy.

There is something about divine perspective that makes it possible for average human beings to endure impossible adversity and accomplish supernatural feats. It took heavenly perspective rooted in faith to motivate and sustain the thousands of people who have laid down their lives for Christ in martyrdom since His resurrection.

Are you facing a hopeless situation in your life or in the life of someone you love? Do you fear death or the uncertainty of tomorrow?

> I don't have to step on any theological or eschatological toes
> to declare the grand finale of our existence boils down to one

word—*worship*. It is God's backstage pass to a whole new realm of vision, power, and authority rooted in intimacy with Him. It isn't complicated. Just take your cue from a little child in a crowded elevator:

"Pick me up, Daddy! I can't see from down here." (p. 195)

Faith, hope, and love seem to be more attainable and accessible when you view them through the eyes of a child. *Does your life appear impossibly complicated at the moment? Do you fear you've accumulated too many mistakes to seek God's face?* You haven't.

Lift your hands to Him right now. Repent of any sins and ask Him for forgiveness. Now cry out to Him and don't worry about what you look like. (I can tell you—you look like a little child crying for Daddy.)

PRAYER

Father, please forgive me for my sins and make me clean again. I can't see from down here. Pick me up, Father, and lift me into heavenly places with You where I belong. Let me see things from Your point of view so my heart will stop pounding and my mind will be free from fear. I love You, praise You, and worship You, Lord.

GodChasers.network is the ministry of Tommy and Jeannie Tenney. Their heart's desire is to see the presence and power of God fall—not just in churches, but on cities and communities all over the world.

How to contact us:

By Mail:

GodChasers.network
P.O. Box 3355
Pineville, Louisiana 71361
USA

By Phone:

Voice: 318.44CHASE (318.442.4273)
Fax: 318.442.6884
Orders: 888.433.3355

By Internet:

E-mail: GodChaser@GodChasers.net
Website: www.GodChasers.net

 # *Join Today*

When you join the **GodChasers.network** we'll send you a free teaching tape!

If you share in our vision and want to stay current on how the Lord is using GodChasers.network, please add your name to our mailing list. We'd like to keep you updated on what the Spirit is saying through Tommy. We'll also send schedule updates and make you aware of new resources as they become available.

Sign up by calling or writing to:

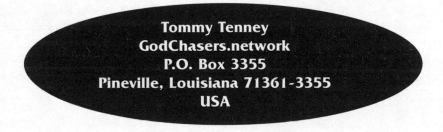

Tommy Tenney
GodChasers.network
P.O. Box 3355
Pineville, Louisiana 71361-3355
USA

318-44CHASE (318.442.4273)
or sign up online at http://www.GodChasers.net/lists/

We regret that we are only able to send regular postal mailings to certain countries at this time. If you live outside the U.S. you can still add your postal address to our mailing list—you will automatically begin to receive our mailings as soon as they are available in your area.

E-mail Announcement List

If you'd like to receive information from us via e-mail, just provide an e-mail address when you contact us and let us know that you want to be included on the e-mail announcement list!

Run With Us!

Become a GodChasers.network Monthly Revival Partner

GodChasers are people whose hunger for Him compels them to run—not walk—towards a deeper and more meaningful relationship with the Almighty! For them, it isn't just a casual pursuit. Traditional Sundays and Wednesdays aren't enough—they need Him everyday, in every situation and circumstance, the good times and bad. Are you a GodChaser? Do you believe the body of Christ needs Revival? If my mandate of personal, National and International Revival is a message that resonates in your spirit, I want you to prayfully consider Running with us! Our Revival Partners fuel GodChasers.network to bring the message of unity and the pursuit of His presence around the world! And the results are incredible, yet humbling. As a Revival Partner, your monthly seed becomes the matches we use to set Revival fires around the globe.

For your monthly support of at least thirty dollars or more, I will send you free, personal fuel each month. This could be audio or videotapes of what I feel the Lord is saying that month. In addition, you will receive discounts on all of our ministry resources. Your Revival Partner status will automatically include you in invitation-only gatherings where I will minister in a more intimate setting.

I rely on our Revival Partners to intercede for the ministry in prayer and even minister with us at GodChaser gatherings around the country. I love to sow seed in peoples' lives and have learned that you can't out give God, He always multiplies the seed! If we give Him something to work with, there's no limit how many He can feed, or how many Revival fires can be started!

Will you run with us every month?

In Pursuit,

Tommy Tenney

Tommy Tenney

Become a Monthly Revival Partner by calling or writing to:

Tommy Tenney/GodChasers.network
P.O. Box 3355
Pineville, Louisiana 71361-3355
318.44CHASE (318.442.4273)

About the Author

TOMMY TENNEY is the author of the bestselling series *The GodChasers*, *God's Favorite House*, *The God Catchers*, and *God's Eye View*. Adding to that series now are *How to Be a God Chaser and a Kid Chaser*, coauthored with his mother, and *Chasing God, Serving Man*, a revelatory revisiting of the story of Mary and Martha. He is also the author of another series of books on unity that includes *God's Dream Team*, *Answering God's Prayer*, and *God's Secret to Greatness*.

Tommy spent ten years pastoring and has spent over twenty years in itinerant ministry, traveling to more than forty nations. He speaks in over 150 venues each year sharing his heart with many thousands. His two passions are *The Presence of God* and *Unity in the Body of Christ*. To help others pursue these twin passions, he founded the GodChasers.network, a ministry organized to distribute his writing and speaking through various mediums. Tommy is a prolific author with more than one million books in print each year, and eight bestselling titles to date. His books have been translated into more than thirty languages.

Three generations of ministry in his family heritage have given Tommy a unique perspective on ministry. He has a gifting to lead hungry people into the presence of God. He and his wife, Jeannie, understand the value of intimacy with God and humility in serving God's people.

The Tenneys reside in Louisiana with their three daughters and two Yorkies.

Notes

WEEK 1

1. 2 Corinthians 4:8–9.
2. See 2 Corinthians 9:6–11 for God's eye view on giving and His abundant supply to "sowers" in the area of finances and virtually every other area of life.
3. See Hebrews 13:5.
4. Genesis 3:15 NLT.
5. Revelation 1:17–18.
6. Isaiah 40:8.
7. God is actively looking for worshipers (see John 4:23).
8. The official term for the problem with the Hubble Space Telescope's (HST) primary mirror was that it was "spherically aberrated." In any case, the HST was fitted with a "contact lens" to correct the problem and restore clear vision. Adapted from data supplied by NASA-Office of Space Science Applications at http://nssdc.gsfc.nasa.gov/nmc/tmp/1990-037B.html.
9. Tommy Tenney, *The God Chasers* (Shippensburg, PA: Destiny Image Publishers, Inc., 1998), pp. 22–23.
10. Isaiah 40:31.
11. Hebrews 10:26–27.
12. See 1 Timothy 2:8.

WEEK 2

1. Colossians 2:9.
2. Watchman Nee, *Christ: The Sum of All Spiritual Things* (New York: Christian Fellowship Publishers, Inc., 1973). Regardless of our individual views on Watchman Nee, we must admit that the title of this book seems to be a unique rephrasing of the passage in Colossians 2.
3. See Philippians 3:8–9.
4. The extent of John's "Jesus addiction" may have even provoked Peter to a touch of jealousy or at least a measure of insecurity (see John 13:23; 21:20–24). The same problem often occurs today when God Chasers openly pursue the presence of the Lord with little or no regard for the disapproval of other people.
5. I deal with this concept and with God's love and the compassionate response of Christian people to the devastation and tragedy experienced by the victims, rescuers, their families, and the American people on September

11, 2001, in my book *Trust and Tragedy: Encountering God in Times of Crisis* (Nashville, TN: Thomas Nelson Publishers, 2001).

6. 2 Corinthians 12:9.
7. See Genesis 18:13–15; 21:1–3 (Sarah and Abraham); Genesis 25:21 (Rebekah and Isaac); and Genesis 29:31; 30:22–24 (Rachel and Jacob).
8. See Joshua 6:25; Matthew 1:5.
9. See Matthew 1:18–25.
10. See Exodus 4:14. It seems God has heard or anticipated every excuse we can produce, so we shouldn't even bother to give Him excuses. "Yes, Lord," will do just fine.
11. Luke 9:23.
12. See Colossians 1:16 and Revelation 4:11.
13. See Exodus 2:11–14; 3:9–11.
14. See Matthew 26:31–35; John 21:15–19.
15. See John 4:23.
16. Isaiah 40:31.
17. 1 Peter 5:5–6.
18. Psalm 51:17.
19. Adapted in part from information provided in the article, "Lincoln, Abraham." Microsoft® Encarta® Online Encyclopedia 2001, at http://encarta.msn.com (21 March 2000).

WEEK 3

1. According to Psalm 22:3, God *inhabits* the praises of Israel (and of His blood-bought people).
2. 1 Thessalonians 5:19 says, "Do not quench the Spirit."
3. This may sound like a radical statement, but it is totally in line with the letter and spirit of the Ten Commandments, the Psalms, with Jesus' statements about what His Father personally seeks for in (worshipers), and with the clear statements given to John in the book of Revelation.
4. See Matthew 22:37.
5. Matthew 10:7–8.
6. See Mark 16:17–18.
7. John 14:12.
8. See Luke 9:23 and John 14:15, respectively.
9. See Psalm 69:9 and John 2:17.
10. I fully understand that God made each of us unique, and that some of us are naturally jovial or openly expressive while others are naturally more *reserved* in nature. Yet God's Word applies to each of us without exception:

we are to be "fervent in spirit," to "have fervent love" for one another, and above all, to stay true to our *First Love* (see Romans 12:11; 1 Peter 4:8; and Revelation 2:4, respectively).

11. Psalm 68:1.
12. John 12:32 KJV.
13. John 3:1–2.
14. See John 7:50.
15. See John 19:39.

WEEK 4

1. John 5:36.
2. John 15:24 NIV.
3. See Acts 2:38–41.
4. See 1 Timothy 6:15–16.
5. See Galatians 4:6.
6. See Matthew 6:8.
7. See John 4:23.
8. See Matthew 6:9–13 and James 5:16.
9. See Romans 12:1.
10. See 2 Timothy 3:5.

WEEK 5

1. See 1 Peter 5:8; Revelation 12:10.
2. See John 8:44 NIV.
3. 1 Peter 5:8.
4. See John 4:24.
5. 1 John 1:8–9.
6. See Philippians 3:9.

WEEK 6

1. Psalm 34:3, emphasis added.
2. Ephesians 1:23.
3. Job 3:25.

WEEK 7

1. See Judges 15:17–19.
2. See 1 Peter 5:6–7.

WEEK 8

1. See Romans 2:11 KJV.
2. Strong, *Strong's Exhaustive Concordance of the Bible,* Moriah (Hebrew #4179, #7200). I do not profess to be a linguist or an expert in Near East and biblical languages such as Hebrew and Aramaic. I based my opinion upon the context of these Bible passages, the unfolding of God's redemptive plan through His Son, Jesus Christ, and James Strong's detailed definition word list for the root word *ra'ah* (#7200), one of the words used in the compound construction of the word *Moriah*.
3. John 8:56, emphasis added.
4. Romans 12:1, emphasis added.

WEEK 9
1. Revelation 5:4–5, emphasis added.
2. Psalm 78:61.
3. See 2 Corinthians 12:9.
4. Ephesians 2:4–6, emphasis added.

BOOKS BY

Tommy Tenney

THE GOD CHASERS

$12.00 plus $4.50 S&H

What is a God Chaser? A person whose hunger exceeds his reach...a person whose passion for God's presence presses him to chase the impossible in hopes that the uncatchable might catch him.

The great GodChasers of the Scripture—Moses, Daniel, David—see how they were driven by hunger born of tasting His goodness. They had seen the invisible and nothing else satisfied. Add your name to the list. Come join the ranks of the God Chasers.

GOD'S EYE VIEW

$23.00 plus $4.50 S&H

In this simple but powerful book, worship will teach you "throne zone" secrets. The higher you go in worship, the bigger God appears (and the smaller your problems seem). If you can't see that from where you are presently sitting, there is a better seat available. The angels will usher you to your reserved seat in "heavenly places" and you will have *God's Eye View*.

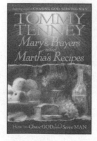

CHASING GOD, SERVING MAN

$17.00 plus $4.50 S&H

Using the backdrop of Bethany and the house of Mary and Martha, Tommy Tenney biblically explores new territory. The revolutionary concepts in this book can change your life. You will discover who you really are (and unlock the secret of who "they" really are)!

MARY'S PRAYERS & MARTHA'S RECIPES

$18.00 plus $4.50 S&H

There are a lot of prayer books and many great spiritual books but there are precious few prayer and compassion books that are practical workbooks as well. Mary's Prayers and Martha's Recipes will be your own special resource for both seasons in your life.

We must learn to work like Martha and worship like Mary. It is essential that we do not do one to the exclusion of the other. It takes the loving service of Martha and the adoring prayers of Mary to complete the full ministry of the Body of Christ in this world.

GodChasers.network
P.O. Box 3355, Pineville, Louisiana 71361-3355
318-44CHASE (318.442.4273)
www.GodChasers.net

VIDEOTAPE ALBUMS BY

Tommy Tenney

FOLLOW THE MAN ON THE COLT
Video $20.00 plus $4.50 S&H

From humility to authority.... If we learn to ride the colt of humility, then we qualify to ride on the stallion of authority.

(This new video helps us understand that we all start this journey crawling—which strenghthens us to walk—that empowers us to run—and rewards us to ride!) Enjoy this great teaching by Tommy Tenney on following the Man on the colt. It will change the way you see the obstacles put in your path! Remember, there is never a testimony without a test!

BROWNSVILLE WILDFIRE SERIES, VOL. 1
"Born to Be a Worshiper"
Video $20.00 plus $4.50 S&H

God would rather hear the passionate praises of His children than the perfection of heavenly worship. It isn't about how good we are as singers, or how skilled we are as musicians. It isn't about singing catchy choruses with clever words. It's all about GOD, and if we'll let our guard down and allow ourselves to truly worship Him, we'll find that He's closer than we ever imagined. If you've been born into God's kingdom, then you were born to be a worshiper! It's time to do the very thing that we were created for!

TURNING ON THE LIGHT OF THE GLORY
Video $20.00 plus $4.50 S&H

Tommy deals with turning on the light of the glory and presence of God, and he walks us through the necessary process and ingredients to potentially unleash what His Body has always dreamed of.

GOING HOME FROM A FUNERAL
Video ~~$20.00~~ $10.00 plus $4.50 S&H

Our country is now in a crisis. Some things will never be the same. Our national mentality is as if we are "going home from a funeral." We are no longer in the orderly, controlled funeral procession. Cars have scattered, taking their own routes back to individual homes and routines. The lights are off and reality hits.

GodChasers.network
P.O. Box 3355, Pineville, Louisiana 71361-3355
318-44CHASE (318.442.4273)
www.GodChasers.net

Catch Him!

The God Catchers	The God Catchers Workbook	Experiencing His Presence
ISBN 0-7852-6710-7	ISBN 0-7852-6623-2	ISBN 0-7852-6619-4

Why do some believers experience genuine, life-changing, personal revival while others don't? In *The God Catchers* and its companions, *The God Catchers Workbook* and the devotional *Experiencing His Presence,* Tommy explains the difference: "God in a sense plays hide and seek. But like a loving parent, He always makes sure He can be found by those who take the time to look." Simply put, those who earnestly seek God rather than wait for something to happen find Him. Full of biblical and contemporary accounts of believers who chased God and caught Him, these three books will motivate readers to discover the joy of finding God and having a loving relationship with Him.

Look for all of these books at your local bookstore,
or by visiting the Web site www.ThomasNelson.com
or calling 1-800-441-0511.

God's Eye View

In *God's Eye View*, Tommy Tenney explores how worship lifts us up to see the trouble we face from God's perspective instead of being trapped in an earthly, time-bound viewpoint. The higher we go, the smaller our problems seem. Tenney also teaches the Principle of Magnification: The closer you get to something, the bigger it appears. In other words, worship not only "shrinks" our problems; it also magnifies God in our lives and to others.

Worship doesn't really change our problems; it just minimizes their influence over us as we focus on God. He doesn't promise to remove all of our circumstances, but God does assure us that in His presence and from His perspective—we can see things as they really are and not how they appear to be.

Higher than a bird's eye view, higher than a man's eye view is God's eye view.

ISBN 0-7852-6560-0

Trust and Tragedy

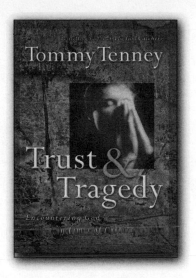

When tragedy strikes you or those around you, the desperate hunt for hope in the secular forest will be futile. The hunters invariably go home empty-handed and broken-hearted because humanity doesn't have the answers. Jesus gave us the key in one of the most direct and unequivocal statements ever made. "I am the way, the truth, and the life. No one comes to the Father except through Me" (John 14:6). Trust and Tragedy is a signpost. On the way, through the truth, to the life. If life is what you need, trust in God will take you there. With articulate words, Tommy Tenney helps lead us past tragedy to that place of trust. After reading this book, you will know what to do and know what to say.

Look for this book at your local bookstore,

or by visiting the Web site www.ThomasNelson.com

ISBN 0-7852-6466-3